133.91   HP3

Lincolnshire
COUNTY COUNCIL

COMMUNITIES, CULTURAL SERVICES
and ADULT EDUCATION
**This book should be returned on or before
the last date shown below.**

0 2 MAY 2011		
1 2 JUN 2011		
1 8 SEP 2011		
0 2 JUN 2014		
2 2 JAN 2015		
1 3 APR 2015		
1 5 APR 2017		
2 2 FEB 2018		

To renew or order library books please telephone 01522 782010
or visit www.lincolnshire.gov.uk
You will require a Personal Icentification Number.
Ask any member of staff for this.

EC. 199 (LIBS): RS/L5/19

D0264611

DEREK ACORAH

EXTREME PSYCHIC

HARPER
element

HarperElement
An Imprint of HarperCollins*Publishers*
77–85 Fulham Palace Road,
Hammersmith, London W6 8JB

The website address is: www.thorsonselement.com

and *HarperElement* are trademarks of
HarperCollins*Publishers* Ltd

First published by HarperElement 2007

3

A catalogue record of this book is
available from the British Library

ISBN-13 978-0-00-723322-9
ISBN-10 0-00-723322-1

Printed and bound in Great Britain by
Clays Ltd, St Ives plc

This book is proudly printed on paper which contains wood
from well-managed forests, certified in accordance with
the rules of the Forest Stewardship Council.
For more information about FSC,
please visit www.fsc-uk.org

Mixed Sources
Product group from well-managed
forests and other controlled sources
www.fsc.org Cert no. SW-COC-1806
© 1996 Forest Stewardship Council

To Christine and Alan –
two of my dearest friends

Contents

Acknowledgements

I would first like to thank my wife Gwen for being the lovely person she is and more importantly for her tireless effort and the hours of hard work she has put into helping me to write all my books to date.

I would also like to thank Ray Rodaway, my tour manager, for his continued hard work and friendship. When the going gets tough along the way, I know I can count on Ray.

A big thank you to my agent, Stuart Hobday, as always working for me behind the scenes without complaint.

I am also indebted to Lizzie Hutchins and all the people at HarperElement for their hard work and support in producing my books.

Acknowledgements

A big thank you to everybody at LIVINGtv for their continued support of my spiritual work, and to Paul Flexton and all the people at Ruggie Media who have worked with me on *Derek Acorah's Ghost Towns* and other projects.

My gratitude goes to all those people up and down the country who come to see me in theatres, who support my work and who are enlightened enough to know the truth. And a huge thank you to Linda and her husband David for their tireless work in running the Derek Acorah Fan Club, bringing many of these wonderful people together to create a big happy family.

Last but not least I would like to thank my lovely mum, Lily. Without her bringing me into the world, this and my other books would not have been written and there would of course have been no Derek.

Introduction

I have been following my spiritual pathway for many years now and have learned to trust implicitly the word and strength of spirit in the many and varied situations I have found myself in. Once I would go on an investigation and merely talk about the energies I was picking up and the spirit entities present, but now I have progressed to channelling those spirit energies.

My experiences in spirit investigation, or 'ghost hunting', as some people call it, date back to the mid-nineties. Some of these investigations have surprised me, some have saddened me and I have learned a great deal from the personalities I have channelled. There have been some experiences, however, that have scared me and taken me to a point where I wondered whether I would come out alive, or at least sane, and it is those experiences I wish to share with you in this book.

I could not have come through these experiences without the trust I have in the strength of my spirit guide Sam and the guardians and doorkeepers who have protected me to the highest degree in some of the more dangerous investigations in which I have taken part. Our guides are our spiritual strength. They inspire us and guide us through hazardous, dangerous and hurtful situations, taking care to ensure that we experience only what is meant for us on our pathway through physical life. Our guardians and doorkeepers prevent intrusion from uninvited negative spirit influences; they draw close to us when necessary and retreat when their presence is not required.

I was horrified once when I heard a well-known sensitive state during a television programme that he 'strengthened up his guides' before entering what he considered to be a potentially hazardous area of the location where he was filming. I can state quite categorically that it is not up to us – or possible for us – to do this. We may, however, *request* the presence of our guides and doorkeepers by offering up a prayer of invocation prior to any situation where we feel we may need their particular help and guidance.

Prior to an investigation I always ask for my guides' and doorkeepers' help and protection for myself and the people around me. I must stress, however, that it is up to each person to be responsible for their own spiritual safety. If they enter into a situation in the knowledge that there is the potential for spirit activity, whether of a positive or negative nature, then they must ask their own guides and inspirers for protection. It is foolhardy to do otherwise and it is very wrong to expect another person to take on that responsibility, whether that person is a medium or not. An individual cannot rely on somebody else and then feign ignorance at a later date, especially if that person is well aware, prior to the investigation taking place, of the possibility of a less than friendly spirit presence being at a location.

Some spirits are very far from friendly, as these pages will show, but all can be encouraged to find their way to their home in the world of spirit.

CHAPTER ONE

Teenage Terror

I was still a teenager when I first experienced the dangerous edge of spirit energies. It was also the first time I *actively* used my psychic powers. At the age of 15 I had been apprenticed to Liverpool Football Club under the management of my eternal hero Bill Shankly. I was now 17 and had completed my apprenticeship. I was a full-time professional footballer playing for Liverpool Football Club 'A' team.

Each week we would play football matches against other clubs' 'A' teams, one of which was Blackburn Rovers. The games against Blackburn were always played at the grounds of a local mental care institution commonly referred to as 'the asylum' in those days.

Whilst the games were being played, certain of the inmates were allowed to watch from the sidelines. The people were of mixed ages, ranging from young adults to quite elderly men and women. One of the regular spectators was David, a strapping young man aged around 21 or 22 years. It did not matter what the weather was like, David would always be there to cheer the Liverpool side on.

I recall one occasion when we were about 15 minutes into the game and the ball went out of play. I took the throw-in, sending the ball in the direction of Peter Price, a former Welsh schoolboy international who was now also a full-time pro with Liverpool. Peter clipped the ball to Ray Witham, our full-back, who in turn hammered it way upfield to our winger, Stephen Peplow. He in turn drove the ball towards the goal-mouth. Up went Ted McDougall to score the first of six goals for our team on that day.

As each goal was scored the audience went into a frenzy of laughter and applause. The atmosphere was alight with excitement and there were a few minor scuffles between the opposing fans. Once such scene involved David. A ball once more went out of play just at the point where David was standing. As he darted forward to retrieve it, one of the female inmates also swooped down to pick it up. Mayhem followed as the two of them fought and pushed one another in an effort to take possession of the ball. It became so bad that they had to be separated and calmed down.

At the end of the game the players would be taken to a part of the building where there were over a dozen baths in a line in the longest bathroom you could ever imagine. David knew the routine and would hang around waiting to speak to the players, even though he should have joined the other inmates as they were taken back to their quarters. Nevertheless, he would wait to chat to us as we came out after our bath and would walk with us towards the coach waiting to take us back home.

I felt very sorry for David. He seemed to be an intelligent lad and although he was a few years older than me, I felt a certain empathy with him and used to make a point of having a chat about what had happened in the game and about Liverpool Football Club's premier team's progress in general.

On this particular day I had completed my bath quite quickly and was making my way down the corridor to the room where we were given tea and sandwiches when I heard a voice call my name. It was David.

'Hi, Derek, mate,' he said. 'Can I share your sandwiches with you? I'm starving. They don't feed me enough here. I'm a growing lad and I need my vitamins.'

We both laughed at this comment, because it was obvious from David's size and stature that he was far from underfed. He accompanied me to the tearoom door and I went in, got myself a plate of sandwiches and a cup of tea and brought them out to him. I have never seen food disappear so quickly in all my life!

When the sandwiches were finished David told me in a confidential manner that he really should not be in that part of the building but should in fact be in the adjoining part where he had his own room. He told me that he had been a resident at the institution for nearly three years.

I asked him why he was there, because apart from appearing to be a little slow, he seemed perfectly normal to me. He informed me that the doctors had told his family that he was mad because he could see and hear people that no one else could. He said he hated the fact that the doctors gave him medicine in an effort to stop him from seeing what they referred to as 'imaginary people'. In order to stay on the right side of the medical staff he even told them that he no longer saw or heard those people. Then he laughed and winked at me and said, 'But I still do!'

As David related this tale to me I felt myself grow cold. The experiences he was describing were exactly the type of thing that I myself experienced and, according to my grandmother, would in later years play a huge part in my life.

From the age of six I had seen and heard people in the world of spirit. Although at that time it did not play a major part in my life, this ability was always with me. I thanked my lucky stars that my grandmother, a medium herself, had recognized what was happening to me. If I had been born into a different family I could quite easily have ended up in a situation similar to the one that David had found himself in and would not have been able to fulfil my dream of playing football professionally for Liverpool Football Club.

My heart went out to David. Just being in his company and close to his aura told me that a grave error had been made – something that was more common-place in those days. The young man was neither mentally deranged nor schizophrenic. Quite simply David had the gift of spirit communication.

David continued speaking. 'Since I've been here I've seen and spoken to lots of people who used to live here but have now died. Sometimes at night before I go to sleep they come and again in the morning when I wake up. It's real, Derek, honest it is!'

I asked David whether he knew of anybody in his family who had had similar experiences. He told me that his father's grandmother had been taken away because she was crazy and had been locked up some-where, never to be seen again by their family. I doubted very much that the poor old lady had been 'crazy'. It was obvious to me that she had passed her gifts down through the family to her great-grandson.

'Do you have to go straightaway, Derek?' David asked me. 'I'd like to show you my room. I can sneak you in there without being seen.'

I hesitated momentarily then said, 'OK, come on then! Let's go!'

David led me down various corridors until we came to what appeared to be a communal sitting room.

Through another door we went and then into another short corridor with a number of doors. David stopped outside one of the doors and opened it. 'This is my room,' he told me proudly.

It was a very plain room with a single bed and a bedside locker. There was a small wardrobe and a couple of shelves. A number of Liverpool Football Club posters adorned the walls. I could only imagine David's loneliness in spending much of his life in this solitary room.

As I approached the window to look out of it I heard a loud bang. I looked down to the floor and saw a box that had moments earlier been sitting on one of the shelves.

'Did you see that, Derek?' David asked me excitedly. 'Did you see the box move? That was Jim! You can't see him, but he's standing right there.' He pointed to a spot just next to the shelves. 'That was naughty, Jim,' he said. 'That was bad!'

I looked towards the place at which David was pointing. I felt a sharp pain in my back and then noticed a man in spirit, small in stature and aged I would say in his early fifties.

'Can you see him, Derek?' David asked me excitedly.

'Yes, I can, David,' I replied and described the spirit man who had joined us in the room.

'Yes, that's him! You can actually see him?' David questioned, his eyes bright with excitement. 'He lived here with us, but he died just over a year ago.'

'And he suffered with a very painful back, didn't he?' I said, ruefully rubbing the area where I had experienced the sharp pain.

'Yes, he did!' David agreed.

David was almost jumping up and down on the spot in his excitement at me being able to see the spirit person who had been his constant visitor for almost 12 months.

There was a small rustling noise in the corner. 'Milly's here too,' said David. 'I liked Milly. She was like a mother to me.'

Poor David. In the three years he had been in this place he had lost two of the people he had grown close to.

I felt a cool breeze play around my body and then suddenly there she was. Milly was a rather stout-looking lady of around 65 to 70 years with white hair and a lovely warm but mischievous smile.

I stood in David's room watching Jim and Milly display their obvious affection towards David. Suddenly I became aware of a feeling that was totally different from the warmth emanating from these two spirit people. I asked David what was in the adjoining room.

David seemed to shrink with fear. 'I don't want to go in there, Derek,' he said. 'There's a nasty man in there and I keep well away from him.'

I asked whether I could go into the room for a moment.

'You can go, but I'm not,' said David hesitantly. 'Please don't ask me to go in there with you.'

I know now that what I was about to do was foolhardy in the extreme. Although I was aware of the spiritual system of things in that I knew of my spirit guide Sam, at that time he had not drawn close to me and introduced himself. I knew nevertheless that he would be by my side. I was also aware that Milly, the old spirit lady, was following close on my heels. She was worried, though. 'Be careful,' I heard her say. 'Don't try to deal with things that you know nothing about.'

Being young and foolish, I paid no heed to Milly's warning and opened the door to the next room. As I entered, I felt a sudden swooping rush of air and saw the spirit form of a man rushing towards me. The force of his energy pinned me against the wall. I felt as though he was towering over me. I could feel the venom of his emotion as he swore and cursed and called me terrible names. I heard a loud shout and realized that it was me crying out in horror. I gabbled desperately, trying to explain that I meant no harm to this tormented soul who wanted to wreak revenge for what he had suffered whilst incarcerated in the institution.

Slowly I felt myself become calmer – more empowered. I knew that my guides and guardians were drawing closer to me in protection. I had put myself in a terribly dangerous situation, but they were there to help me.

The spirit man's raving calmed down and he backed slowly away from me. He seemed to realize that I was no threat to him.

'What is your name?' I asked him.

He said nothing, merely glowered at me from across the room.

I heard Milly's voice. 'His name's Alex,' she said, 'and he was here for years and years – even before I arrived. He suffered some terrible things in the name of treatment. We all did, but it affected Alex more. In the end he got the opportunity and he hanged himself. Me and Jim have been trying to coax him to come over to the light side, but he's afraid that things will be bad for him – that he'll be hurt again. Pray for him, Derek, and we'll make sure that he comes over to the heavenly side with us.'

I promised that I would do just that.

I went back into David's room and explained to him that both Jim and Milly were going to help the poor suffering soul next door and that he needn't be afraid any longer.

David was looking puzzled. 'You can see Jim and Milly and other people just like I can. You can hear them too. Why aren't you in here with me?'

I was moved and saddened by his question. 'I really don't know, David,' I replied.

It was more than time to go. I was already late. When I reached the car park all the other players were waiting on the coach for me. Our team trainer, George Patterson, was very annoyed. 'Where've you been Derek? You're in trouble on Monday! It's right to the boss that you'll be heading.'

I didn't mind. I felt happy and elated. We had won the game 6–1 and with my prayers and the assistance of Milly and Jim, poor tormented Alex would find his way to his rightful placed in the world of spirit.

I occasionally kept in touch with David after I left Liverpool Football Club. I am happy to say that the institution was closed some years later and David was found a home in the community, where he integrated happily. As far as I am aware he is still living a happy and free life.

I often wonder how many people have been mistakenly diagnosed as mentally ill and incarcerated for their supposed 'own good and the good of others' when in fact all they were doing was communicating with the world beyond.

I was looking forward to the seven-week summer break from playing football. Although I loved my life as a professional footballer, it was nice to have a break from the rigorous training regime. Back in the 1960s the wages for footballers were a far cry from the enormous sums commanded today, so it was not unusual for us young players to take summer jobs to put a few extra pounds into our pockets. The previous year I had taken a job as a football coach at a Pontins Holiday Camp, but this year I did not feel inclined to play at being 'Uncle Derek' to a camp full of aspiring young football players and wanted to take the time off to relax and enjoy myself.

My friends Vinny and Frank planned to take a trip south to visit Vinny's aunt, who lived in Langley, near Slough, for a week. They then planned to stay on for a further week at a youth hostel in the area. They asked me whether I would like to join them. I was delighted to accept their offer. Vinny and Frank had been my friends since school, but I did not get much time to spend with them due to my football commitments. This would be an ideal opportunity to catch up on old times and enjoy the company of my friends.

We set off one sunny summer morning, travelling down in Frank's car, which was an enormous old Humber Sceptre. Although the vehicle was old, it still retained its luxurious interior.

After making our stately progress south we arrived at Vinny's aunt's home in the early evening. The next week was spent thoroughly enjoying ourselves as we explored the areas around Hounslow, Egham and Windsor.

When the first week was up we gathered our belongings, thanked Vinny's aunt for putting up with us and moved on to the hostel. It was an old house of enormous proportions, standing in its own grounds.

At one time I suppose it must have been a family home, but now it was given over to offering cheap accommodation and sporting activities to youngsters such as myself and my friends who wanted a cheap, clean and cheerful holiday environment away from our parents.

I have to say that the hostel was not quite what I expected, but I settled in nevertheless. The food was good and wholesome and the communal areas offered table tennis, television and snooker. The bedrooms, however, were in fact dormitories, with six single beds to each room. Next to each bed stood a metal locker/wardrobe in which we could secure our belongings during the time we were out of the hostel either exploring the surrounding area or taking advantage of the activities on offer.

Although I had never stayed in a large old house before, I thought nothing of it as I settled down for the night. The only strange thing was going to bed with so many other people in the same room.

On the first night I suppose I must have been asleep for a couple of hours or more when I was jolted awake by a loud banging noise which seemed to be coming from the metal cabinet next to my bed.

15

'Did anyone hear those banging noises?' I whispered out into the darkened room.

A couple of voices answered me from the beds containing lads I did not know, saying, 'That's Sparky messing about. Take no notice.'

Apparently 'Sparky' was a young man who was also staying at the hostel and who enjoyed playing practical jokes on the other residents. It was his practice to creep along to a room and pull the covers off people or reach inside the doorway to flash the lights on and off, then beat a hasty retreat back to the room in which he was sleeping.

Satisfied with this explanation, Vinny and Frank settled back down to sleep, but I was not so sure about it. I could sense psychically that there was more to the banging than met the eye.

I turned on my bedside light and was amazed to notice a large indentation in the door of the cabinet next to my bed which I was sure had not been there before. I turned the light off once more and lay there listening to the deep breathing of my bedroom companions and the creaks and groans of the old house. Sensing nothing untoward, though, I eventually drifted off to sleep once more.

The following morning Vinny, Frank and I made our way down to the kitchen area where we would eat our breakfast. The cook, Mrs Marsden, was a kindly lady who fed us well, but you could tell immediately that she would stand no nonsense from anyone staying at the hostel. As she was clearing away our plates, she asked what we planned to do that day. We told her that we were going down to the stables to take part in a trek around the area. 'Well, you be careful, lads,' she told us.

I wanted to ask her about the room in which we were staying, but because she seemed such a no-nonsense woman I thought that I had better keep my questions to myself, especially as they might get 'Sparky' into trouble.

We returned to the hostel later that evening with very sore legs and feeling extremely tired. After our dinner and a gentle game of snooker we decided to turn in early.

We all fell asleep more or less immediately and were not disturbed by the arrival of the other three residents of the room. But we had only been asleep for around three hours when we were startled awake by the sound of a loud scream echoing around the room.

We all switched our bedside lights on simultaneously and were shocked to see one of the lads in the other beds sitting up holding his face and looking absolutely terrified. We asked him what had happened and he told us that he had decided to flout the rules and have a cigarette in bed before going off to sleep – something that was definitely against the rules. He explained that as he was puffing away on his cigarette it had suddenly been snatched out of his mouth by what he described as 'the shadowy figure of a man' who had then turned the lit end of the cigarette around and jabbed it into the side of his face.

We all rushed over to him and sure enough, there on his left cheek was a small round burn mark. Everyone went very quiet. I remembered the previous evening and the loud bang which had resulted in the indentation of my wardrobe door. I was positive that there was a negative spirit presence in the room and I was determined, come what may, to get to the bottom of the matter.

Needless to say, not much sleeping went on in the room that night as we all sat up talking about what had happened. I did not like to air my own views on the matter to my bedroom companions. I was just 19 and was afraid that the lads I was with would make fun of me if I started talking in depth about spirit activity.

The following morning I tentatively asked Mrs Marsden whether any strange things had ever happened in the room in which my friends and I were staying. She looked at me long and hard and asked why I would ask such a question. I told her that there had been a couple of disturbing incidents over the previous two nights.

'Oh dear!' was her surprising response. 'So it's started up again, has it?'

She told me that many years ago the old house had been used as a hospital for soldiers recovering from injuries and exposure to gas sustained whilst fighting in the trenches during World War I. Many of these men were driven almost mad with the pain of their horrific injuries and amputations. There was a story that she had heard about a man, George Adams, who had suffered terrible burns. He used to lash out in his pain and later, as he slowly recovered, became terrified of fire. The mere thought of anybody putting him in danger by smoking in bed had driven him almost insane with anger and he would attack any poor unfortunate soldier who happened to light up a comforting cigarette anywhere around him. He had actually succumbed to his lung injuries at the old house. For many years after his passing there had been reports that his spirit was wandering around the old house, making his presence felt by banging around on locker doors, and anybody smoking in bed made him very angry.

'I don't know how true the story is,' Mrs Marsden commented, 'but I believe in these things and I suspect you do too, young man.'

I nodded, though again I was unwilling to share my experiences and my grandmother's predictions.

That night we all went to bed after another busy day. Although we lay awake for a while listening and waiting for something to happen, nothing did and we awoke the following morning refreshed after a good night's sleep.

The matter regarding George Adams was still lying heavy on my mind, though. I decided that when night fell and we had all retired to bed I would quietly attempt to communicate with him to try and persuade him to join his loved ones in his rightful place in the world of sprit. I had spent many long hours talking to my grandmother and she had explained to me that sometimes people pass away from this world but, for different reasons, do not pass immediately to the heavenly state. She told me that it was up to people like herself, and indeed me, to help them seek the light by praying and asking their family and guardian angels to come for them and show them the way to their heavenly home.

After another pleasant day and an evening at the cinema watching *Dr Zhivago*, Vinny, Frank and I returned to the hostel. We had a late supper and then retired to bed at around midnight.

We had been asleep for a while when I was wakened by what sounded like thunder. I switched on my bedside lamp and looked at my watch. It was 3.45 a.m. The noise continued, though strangely it began to sound as though it was coming from the walls of the room. Suddenly there was a very loud scraping noise, as though somebody was dragging something over the tiled floor. Just as the other lads in the room woke up and switched on their lights, I saw the dark shadow of a man cross the room.

The others had had enough. 'Come on, Derek!' they shouted as they all hurriedly dressed and ran off down the corridor, I assumed to the communal room.

'I'm coming!' I shouted after them. I had no intention of joining them, however, until I had found out exactly what was going on.

With the room empty I felt free to attempt to communicate with whoever was there. 'Who are you?' I shouted out into the atmosphere. 'Why are you here? Let me see you!'

After I had shouted out my questions once more, the spirit form of a man built up before me. I could see quite clearly the horrible burn injuries to his face. I sensed a great anger with him and I quaked with fear at my audacity in thinking that I could take on such tangible negative energy on my own. I prayed fervently to my guides to help me. I knew that they would surround me and safeguard me, but that did not stop the real fear I was experiencing.

Then suddenly I realized – or was inspired to realize – that the man's anger was not directed towards me personally. He was in fact hurt and afraid. These feelings manifested as anger about his situation. In reality this man did not realize that he had experienced physical death. He thought that he was still living his life here on Earth and was angry and frustrated because he thought that people were ignoring him because of his horrible disfigurement. Added to this was his fear of fires and being burned again.

'But *I* can see you,' I almost pleaded with him. He stopped and looked at me. As calmly as I could I spoke out into the ether. I told him that he must seek the light, that he must make his way to the heavenly state, that he must ignore for a while the living and must follow the bright being who frequently beckoned to him. I told him that it was right and proper that he should make that pleasant journey and live a trouble-free existence with his heavenly family, free from care and pain.

With that I closed my eyes and prayed fervently for him. I called upon his guides and the help of his guardians and family in the heavenly state to guide his footsteps. I also asked my own guides and inspirers to add their strength to my prayers and assist this poor demented soul on his journey.

The atmosphere began to lighten and after a few minutes I knew that George's transition had finally taken place. The room held a feeling of peace and calm – a feeling that it had never had before.

I felt drained. I slowly left the room and went to join my friends in the communal room. 'Everything's quiet now,' I told them. 'Why don't you come back to bed?' Reluctantly, they agreed that they would do just that.

We all had a peaceful night's sleep and for the rest of our stay we were undisturbed.

On our journey home Vinny, Frank and I discussed the events that had taken place. They asked what had happened in the room when I had been in there on my own and I decided to tell them.

They both looked at me strangely before saying in unison, 'You're weird! But we like you!'

We all laughed and the matter was forgotten – at least by them. For me it was just a taste of many more scary situations to come, and on some occasions even my life would be put at risk.

Chapter Two

Horror in my Home Town

My home city of Liverpool is rich in stories of haunted houses and ghostly events. It has seen more than its fair share of events, being not only one of the UK's major cities but also once one of England's most important seaports. During the years when I had an office in the city centre, I was often asked about events taking place in people's homes. If I felt that I could help these people I usually did, and on most occasions it was discovered that the slight disturbances being experienced were the work of people from the spirit world who were in visitation to family members merely to let them know they were around. Occasionally the spirit people would be attempting to warn their loved ones of a wrong decision about to be made or an event about to take place that might cause concern to the family. More often than not, by opening up to the emanations surrounding the querant I could provide answers to their questions via the good offices of Sam. There was one occasion, however, when I felt that a visit to the person's house was in order, as I could pick nothing up in the aura of the young woman concerned that would explain the events she described taking place in her home.

The houses around the Great Georges Street area of Liverpool are large. They were once the homes of the well-to-do and the area was considered highly respectable. Maria lived just around the corner from Great Georges Street in one such house that had been converted into apartments. She had moved into the ground-floor apartment with her husband and her two children – boys aged three and five – approximately six months earlier.

Maria told me that from the time that she and her family had moved into their home she had never felt particularly settled. For some reason she had always felt worried about her children and did not like to leave them alone in any room on their own. Even when they were in bed she felt the urge to keep checking on them to make sure that they were safe, even though she knew that no harm could possibly come to them. Her husband, she told me, was becoming more than a little irritated by her constant checking and nervousness about their two sons, especially as she now refused to go out without them, which had effectively brought to an end the Saturday nights out that they used to enjoy while their sons were in the care of a babysitter. It had reached the point where Maria's nervousness was having a detrimental effect on her marriage. A further house move was out of the question because Maria's husband could find nothing wrong with their home and it had the added bonus of being close to his work in a nearby restaurant. With late working hours, it was simple for him to walk the short distance home rather than have to get a cab.

'Joe thinks it's all rubbish and imaginings,' Maria explained to me, 'and it's true that there's nothing tangible there. Nothing has happened – yet! I feel, though, that before too long things may start to happen and I'm afraid for my two boys.'

I could see that Maria was truly frightened. I could tell that she was a very sensitive soul and was obviously picking up something from the atmosphere of the house in which she lived. I decided that the only way to get any answers for her was to actually visit her home to see what I could find out.

On the appointed day I arrived outside the large old house. As I stood on the doorstep waiting for Maria to answer the bell, I felt a sense of unease overcome me. Just standing there, before I had even entered the house, I knew that something sinister had taken place within the four walls. In spite of obvious renovation over the years, there still remained the ominous presence of death.

As I heard footsteps approaching the front door I whispered a prayer of protection and asked Sam to draw close to me. Almost immediately I felt his reassuring presence and heard his quiet voice reply, 'I'm here, Derek.'

Maria opened the door. As she did so, immediately the feelings that had assailed my senses grew tenfold. I was whisked back in time to the mid-Victorian era. The white painted hallway faded and was replaced by a much darker decoration – brown paint and dark woodwork. The carpeted floor was replaced by a tiled floor with a chequered pattern. Horrifyingly, on the floor lay the body of a woman, horribly butchered – her blood was splattered up the walls and pooled across the floor.

I was snapped back to the present day by Maria's greeting: 'Hello, Derek. Welcome! Do come in.'

I walked into a long passageway with various doors leading off it. These I presumed led to the other rooms in the building. Maria led me along the hallway to the rear of the house and invited me into the kitchen, which looked out onto a relatively small yard area. She introduced me to her friend Val, whom she had invited along for moral support.

Once more, when entering the room, I was taken back in time clairvoyantly. The bright paintwork and stainless steel kitchen equipment had been replaced by a dismal-looking room containing a copper boiler and a huge stone sink. Once upon a time this room had been a scullery of sorts, where laundering of the family's clothes and linen had taken place. Again, the whole place was smeared with blood – it lay in pools on the floor and was smeared on the walls. I looked down and it was even more horrifying – there was the body of a small boy, his head almost severed. Next to him lay a long-bladed knife.

Desperately I fought the feeling of nausea that threatened to overcome me and tried to bring myself back to the present day. The horrific scene began to dissipate and once more I was back in the pleasant, bright modern-day kitchen. I accepted the cup of coffee that Maria was offering me.

I was definitely beginning to understand why a sensitive person such as Maria was finding it difficult living in what should have been a very nice and comfortable home. I asked her where her children were. She told me that she had dropped them off earlier at her mother's home. I was more than pleased to hear that the two lads were safe and away from what could turn out to be a rather difficult situation.

I felt that I would need the concentration and energy of both Maria and Val on this occasion. When we had finished our coffee I asked whether I could go back down the hallway and into the room at the front of the apartment and which looked out over the street.

Maria and Val accompanied me. On opening the door to what was a pleasant and comfortable lounge, again I was whooshed back in time to a room heavy with dark Victoria decoration, gas mantles and solid furniture. Once more my clairvoyant eye took in the horrifying spectacle of murder and carnage. A girl lay bleeding profusely on the floor. Close by the body of another boy – a little older than the one in the kitchen – lay slumped by the ornate fireplace. My ears rang with the screams and cries of the four victims who had passed on to the world of spirit so horrifically more than 100 years earlier. I was sickened by the sound of a knife hacking and slashing through flesh and bone. The acrid smell of blood hung heavy in the air.

Up to this point in time I had merely viewed the horrific aftermath of a mass murder, the emanations of which hung in the atmosphere due, I knew, to the regular spirit return of the perpetrator of the horrendous crime. After a few moments of standing in the room opening myself up further to the terrible emanations I began to detect a spirit presence. A young man began to emerge from the ether. He was not tall – around 5 feet, 6 inches – and was of stocky build. His dark hair, though covered by a hat, hung down the sides of his face and he wore a dark coat with light-coloured trousers. He had a wild expression upon his face and his hands hung down limply by his sides. They were covered in the blood of his victims.

I sensed an evil in the spirit of the man standing before me – an evil combined with a complete lack of feeling for anything or anybody. When on the Earth plane, he had been a deranged soul willing to do anything to earn himself a few shillings. I had the impression that he had once been connected in some way to the sea. I felt that somehow he had inveigled himself into this house and had dispatched the occupants with no more feeling or compassion than one would have in swatting a fly.

I prayed once more silently to Sam. Again I heard him whisper close by me, 'I'm here.'

I knew that I had to rid the home of the evil the spirit man had brought with him. Sam's voice told me, 'He did not escape man's justice – he was hanged for his crimes. He is John – John Wilson. Now he needs to face spiritual justice so that he can progress and find his proper place in the spirit world.'

I had not come equipped to perform a candle rite to clear the atmosphere of a spirit's presence, as I had not dreamed that I would require such radical action when I had set out that morning. I hoped that Maria would be able to help. I could see from the surroundings that she had a number of candles.

In order not to unduly frighten the two young women I quietly asked Maria whether she could help by providing a white cloth, two bowls – one filled with salt and one with water – and seven candles – three green and four white. I was relieved when she said that she could. She left the room.

John was still standing watching me, his eyes flickering to the left and the right, with a sneering expression on his face. 'You won't get rid of me, Derek Acorah!' he stated in a contemptuous voice. 'I like it here! Two more nice little boys! Oh, how the knife slices so easily through soft young flesh!'

I was sickened by his statement. I remembered Maria's two young sons and realized that the two murdered children would have been around the same age.

'Henry and Alfred had such sweet young flesh,' I heard John say. He gave an evil cackle. 'I have the power of the master behind me!'

'Not for very much longer,' I thought to myself. I realized now that John Wilson assumed he was in league with the devil. Didn't he realize that no such person or creature existed – that 'the devil' was merely man's personification of all things evil?

I heard Maria returning from the kitchen. Val opened the door for her and she carried in a tray with the two small bowls of salt and water, a white cloth and the seven candles on it.

John Wilson viewed the contents of the tray with interest. His horrible laughter once more echoed around the room.

I cleared the coffee table in the middle of the room, reached for the white cloth and put it on it. John's eyes narrowed as he watched me. He moved a little nearer to where I was standing.

Next I reached into the bowls and sprinkled the cloth first with a little of the salt and then with some water. At that a great whoosh of energy sent the cloth flying from the table and onto the floor. I bent down to pick it up and replace it once more upon the table. Then there was another surge of energy and I felt the not insignificant presence of John Wilson all around me, trying to overshadow and overpower me. My breath felt as though it had been sucked from my lungs and I struggled to breathe. I could not under any circumstances allow myself to lose consciousness – it was imperative that I remained aware and did not lose control.

'Put the cloth on the table,' I struggled to tell the terrified women. 'Place the bowls on the cloth and line up the candles – green at the front and white behind.'

I felt as though I was being pummelled repeatedly by unseen fists and prayed to Sam and my guardians to help me. I knew that they were there empowering me.

'Light the candles,' I almost screamed to Maria, 'and pray – say the Lord's Prayer – anything!'

'Our Father who art in heaven …' I heard the women begin the familiar words. I joined my voice to theirs, though it was little more than a croak. Then I reached out and grabbed Val's hand. As I did so, I felt the energy that was attempting to overpower me relinquish its hold a little.

I stretched out and took Maria's hand. 'Hold hands! Hold hands and continue!' I instructed, by now feeling more in control of the situation.

As Maria and Val repeated the hallowed words I prayed fervently for peace to be brought to this home and for the spirit of John Wilson to be taken to the place where he could commence his journey to redemption for his sins against innocent people. Slowly, slowly, I felt his spirit power weaken and eventually fail as the energies of goodness overcame him and he was led by his own guides to the place where he could begin the long process of atoning for his sins.

The flames of the candles flickered. We continued our prayers. Finally, a wonderful peace and calm pervaded the atmosphere. I knew my work was done.

I looked at Maria and Val. They were standing with their eyes tight shut, still holding hands. 'Do you feel anything?' I asked them.

Visibly relaxing, they opened their eyes and looked around. 'I feel warmth and lightness,' said Maria. 'It's something I've never felt here before.'

'The spirit influence causing your problems has gone now,' I explained. 'He was a vicious and unhappy soul who once had a connection with this home.'

I did not want to frighten Maria by giving her the details of mass murder that I had witnessed. It was sufficient that she now felt happier and at peace in her home.

After that Maria would occasionally crop by my office in Liverpool to say hello. The problems that she had experienced during the first six months of occupation of her home never returned. I do not know where she is now, whether she is still in that apartment or not, but I am sure that her life since that day has been a happy and progressive one.

CHAPTER THREE

The Condemned Man

Many are the letters I receive from people all over the world telling me of their experiences in connection with the paranormal. It is impossible for me to respond personally to the many letters and e-mails, but I do my best to read them all. Occasionally, if I feel that I can help and if my busy schedule permits, I will contact the person who has written to me and attempt to help them.

One such letter came to me from Anne. Her husband Harry owned a small shop where he sold small electrical goods and hardware just outside Manchester in the Atherton area. Harry had run the shop for many years and in fact had inherited the business from his father.

Anne had included her telephone number in her letter and so I decided that I would contact her. She expanded on what she had briefly outlined in her letter to me – that she and Harry had experienced no problems whatsoever during the years that they had run the shop until one day a friend of hers had asked whether she and some friends could conduct a 'ghost hunt' in the old cellars. The friend, together with four other people, including one who purported to be a 'medium', had spent the night in the cellar.

Anne had been surprised when her friend had regaled her the following day with stories of evil entities and items being thrown around. The friend had even claimed that she had been pushed down the cellar steps.

Neither Anne nor Harry could ever recall experiencing anything untoward in any part of the shop premises. The cellars, although rather cold, had never caused them concern when venturing down there. In fact, they used them as storage space for stock. Consequently, they were frequently up and down the cellar steps, and neither had ever been pushed.

Since the night of the 'ghost hunt', however, both had noticed that the stock in the cellar was being moved around on a regular basis. Once or twice it had looked as though items had been thrown, resulting in some breakages – not something that a small business can afford. The atmosphere in the cellar, and indeed the shop itself, had also changed.

I asked Anne whether she knew what her friend and the group of people had done in the cellar.

'Well, I know that they held a séance,' she replied.

I suspected that I now knew what had happened. Anne's friends had tried to emulate what is frequently seen on paranormal programming these days. They had undoubtedly had sat in a circle and attempted to invoke the spirit world. Unfortunately, they had more than likely done this without taking the necessary precaution of requesting protection for themselves and their surroundings, and they would definitely not have cleared the atmosphere before they left, consequently leaving a portal open and giving any malevolent spirit who wished to enter the cellar a perfect doorway. I doubted very much that the so-called 'medium' had any mediumistic abilities whatsoever. If they had, they would have ensured that complete closure had been achieved before the property had been vacated.

It is not, of course, the responsibility of a medium to provide protection for those who choose to enter a potentially haunted location. That is the responsibility of the individual. Any person who blames a medium for any resultant mishaps after an investigation is merely displaying gross ignorance of the paranormal in general and, in my opinion, displaying personal irresponsibility towards themselves. It has been known for an individual to blame an underlying and genetic health condition on a medium by claiming that 'the medium did not protect them adequately' during an investigation. This is utter rubbish. The person concerned would be better served seeking the advice of a member of the medical profession.

I made an arrangement to travel to Anne and Harry's shop the following Tuesday. On that day, accompanied by Ray Rodaway, my tour manager, I travelled to Atherton and found the shop we were looking for.

As soon as I entered the premises I became aware that the shop had not always served the purpose of retailing hardware but had once dealt in metals of a finer and far more precious variety. I could see jewellery and pocket watches displayed in velvet-lined mahogany and glass cases. The name 'John' rang out and the spirit outline of a small, bustling but well-dressed man formed before me. He was pottering about, polishing a piece here and winding a watch there. He seemed totally oblivious to the fact that the years had moved on and changed the shop and that instead of the precious goods in which he dealt there were now wooden shelves lined with more mundane items such as screws, nails and pots of paint.

Anne took me behind the counter and through a doorway from which an open flight of wooden steps led down to the cellar. As soon as the door was opened I could sense a presence. It was the spirit form of a man lurking in the dark recesses of the cellar. Unlike the busy spirit gentleman in the shop area, this man wore an ugly expression on his face – a mixture of anger, fear and disillusionment.

I reached the bottom of the cellar steps, Ray following close behind me. Anne hovered halfway down, obviously afraid to descend any further. There were a number of large cardboard cartons stacked against one wall and on the floor lay a couple of stepladders. Against another wall were stacked plastic crates full of small boxes of the type that contain nails and drill bits or other such hardware paraphernalia. It was next to these crates that the spirit man stood.

'Who are you?' I shouted.

I received no reply. I edged a little closer. Suddenly a crate seemed to fly to the floor, scattering its contents everywhere.

'William! I'm William!' I clairaudiently heard the man growl. 'Leave me alone!' he commanded.

As I looked at the floor, now covered in small boxes, the impression of a man's body lying in a bloody puddle came to me. I sensed that this man had not met his end as a result of an accident. This was murder!

I looked back at William and stepped a little closer to him.

'I'm not afraid of you, William,' I stated. 'You know you must leave here.'

'I will not! Take these people and go!' he demanded. 'I will stay here with him – Walter.' He pointed towards the area where I had been impressed clairvoyantly with the sight of the bleeding corpse.

'No, you will not, William!' I told him. 'You must go. You must leave these good people in peace.'

The spirit man lunged towards me and I staggered back with the force of his energy.

'Careful, Derek!' I heard Ray's gruff voice behind me and I felt him steady my balance by placing his hand on my arm.

'Just go!' was William's sneering response.

I began to feel quite ill. I had a feeling of nervous sickness in my stomach which almost made me retch. I knew I was picking up the emotions of William immediately prior to his passing from this physical life. I also picked up a sense of loss and hopelessness – a feeling of desolation at being let down. I realized that William had met an untimely end himself.

'Man's justice was meted out to him,' I heard Sam tell me, 'but in William's case it was an injustice. He was innocent of the crime he was accused of. He is afraid to progress to the world of spirit for fear of what will happen to him. Man's justice let him down. He is afraid that spiritual justice will do the same.'

It would be a difficult task, but I knew then that I had to convince William that he had to leave this place to which he had so recently come. It was not right that he should spend eternity with the ghostly body of a man he was accused of killing but in fact had not.

I drew closer to William once more, but again the force of his energy repelled me and I stumbled backwards. Each time I was repelled, however, I recovered myself and moved forward again. I knew that if I could get close to this spirit being I had more chance of convincing him to move away from this dark cellar and progress to the light.

'Talk about Polly,' Sam advised me. 'Tell William she is waiting for him. He has nothing to fear.'

'Polly!' I shouted out. 'Polly's waiting for you.'

When he heard that, the expression on the spirit man's face softened and an all-pervading sadness seemed to surround us. I knew then that this was no evil spirit come to wreak devastation on anyone, but a sad and suffering soul who was afraid to move on to meet his loved ones on the higher side of life.

William had been executed for a murder he did not commit and was frightened of that travesty of justice being repeated in the spirit world. He was afraid that he would have to spend all his time with souls who had not yet atoned for the horrendous deeds they had committed in their physical lives.

Eventually I was standing so close to William he was almost overshadowed by my aura. With a tremendous effort and the greatest depth of feeling and sincerity that I could convey, I pleaded with him to move towards the light.

'Polly is waiting for you. She will meet you and show you the way. You do trust Polly, don't you?'

He nodded. I felt a hesitation and then an enormous rush of spiritual energy, so great that I staggered back and, tripping over one of the ladders, fell heavily to the floor.

Ray rushed forward to help me up. There was a shriek from Anne, who was still standing on the cellar steps. 'I saw a huge flash of white light, Derek!' she cried.

'Did you feel that?' I asked them both.

'I can't feel anything,' they replied.

'Exactly! There's nothing here anymore. Everything is back as it should be,' I told them.

I spent the next 15 minutes or so clearing the atmosphere. No spirit would enter the premises again in order to cause upset and unrest. And I knew that William had entered the world of spirit and was now at peace with his beloved Polly.

CHAPTER FOUR

Black Magic in
Underground Edinburgh

From the mid-nineties right up to 2001 I took part in psychic programmes for Granada Breeze, the satellite arm of Granada Television. This company ceased to broadcast live programming in July 2001 and ceased airing altogether at the end of December 2001.

During my time working at Granada Breeze I took part in programmes such as *The Psychic Zone*, *Livetime* and *Psychic Livetime*, but it was *Predictions with Derek Acorah* that really threw me into the televised psychic investigation arena.

Predictions with Derek Acorah comprised three sections, one of which involved investigating allegedly haunted locations throughout the UK. I would be collected from my home by a producer and her assistant and would then be taken to the chosen location, where we would be met by a camera and sound team. The investigation would then take place with me having no prior knowledge whatsoever of either the location or its history (sound familiar?)!

One such place that I was taken was the city of Edinburgh. Beneath the streets of modern Edinburgh lies another equally large city, a hidden city, known as the Edinburgh Vaults. In years gone by these vaults were inhabited by people who lived their lives underground. There were homes down there, and shops, industry and drinking establishments thrived. Some people even kept animals. It was not unknown for cattle and poultry to spend their lives living under the city streets.

There are many vaults now open to the visitor, Blair Street Vaults and Mary King's Close being those I investigated with the LIVINGtv programme *Most Haunted*, but it was Granada Breeze and *Predictions with Derek Acorah* that first introduced me to the mysteries and horrors of one of Scotland's most famous and beautiful cities.

* * *

Niddry Street Vaults are reached by travelling up Niddry Street itself, which is hardly wide enough to accommodate one vehicle, never mind two. Almost at the top of the street on the right-hand side is a sign proclaiming 'Witchcraft Museum'. It is from here that you gain entry to Niddry Street Vaults.

To the left of the entrance is the museum itself, which is full of the instruments of torture used to extract confessions from those poor unfortunates accused, mostly without basis or proof, of witchcraft. These poor broken victims were then transported to a place where they were burned to death for their supposed crimes.

As I negotiated the steps to the vaults that first time I was made aware of a feeling of persecution – of women suffering at the hands of a nasty misogynistic man. I was sure that these feelings and impressions had nothing to do with the vaults I was about to enter but were the lasting impressions of the history of the tools of torture I had so recently viewed, some of which were authentic and dated back to the seventeenth century, when such atrocities took place.

I went down to a dark passageway, illuminated only by ghostly green lights that had been placed along the wall. Although it was a relatively chilly spring day outside, the temperature underground was surprisingly warm. The floors were covered in puddles of the condensation that was trickling perpetually down the walls. The air smelled stale, though not badly so – much like a room that has remained unopened for a number of years.

The first thing that I encountered on entering the vaults was a closed area to the left of me. On peering through the wrought-iron gateway, I could see that this 'room' was dedicated to some form of pagan worship. There was a pentacle on the floor and the walls were decked out with pagan regalia.

Outside the room there stood a wooden block. 'This was used to chop people's heads off,' the guide who had accompanied us said with some relish. Although it was impressively marked and stained with 'blood', a quick touch told me that this story was untrue. My psychometric senses could pick up no such savagery having taken place anywhere near the block of wood – it had been placed there for effect and was no more than 'window dressing'.

We moved forward along the passageway, visiting each room in turn. The camera rolled and I explained what I was receiving both clairvoyantly and clairaudiently. I picked up on children – lots of children. There were also workmen carrying out their daily workaday lives. In other parts of the vaults there were drinking houses and an air of industry. Each room told a story.

There was one room, however, that was different. This room I knew had been used in a way that none of the other rooms had. In the centre stood a stone circle. The atmosphere within this room held emanations that were not altogether pleasant. If I wanted to uncover the secrets of this vault, however, I would have to return at a later date.

Some four years later I found myself back in Edinburgh. I was there to appear at the Festival Theatre as part of my tour of the UK. What better opportunity was there to revisit the vaults at Niddry Street and delve further into the mysteries of the room containing the stone circle?

Together with Ray Rodaway, I once more descended the well-remembered steps into the vaults themselves.

As I did so, I heard somebody not of this physical world shout out, 'Balfour! Balfour! Alison was innocent!'

I received a momentary clairvoyant image of a woman in her forties. She had two children with her. There was an air if extreme sadness about her, a feeling of loss – of unfinished business on the orders of James VI of Scotland, who was not particularly fond of women and was an ardent supporter of the witchcraft laws. I was later to discover that Alice Balfour had been burned at the stake as a witch. Her husband, also accused of witchcraft, had been beheaded in Germany.

In the vaults everything remained the same – nothing had changed in the time that I had been away. I bypassed the rooms I had previously investigated and headed straight for the vault containing the stone circle.

As we moved along the dimly lit passageway I was aware of hooded spectral figures in a regimented line entering the room to which I was walking. As I entered the room myself, I felt the air temperature grow colder and colder. Ray remarked to me how cold he felt. I felt the same. I was also feeling something else – a predatory watchfulness.

I peered into the gloom of the far corner of the vault and noted the spirit form of a man standing there dressed in a dark robe. He had an air of officialdom about him and I gained the impression of the name 'Alexander'.

As Ray and I stood in the doorway, we heard a sudden noise – a noise that could only be a shower of stones falling to the ground.

'Are you going in, Ackers?' Ray asked. 'Because if you are, be careful – it sounds as though the roof's not as stable as it could be. I heard stones falling just then.'

I asked Ray to stay in the doorway. How I wished we had thought to bring a torch along with us, as the only lighting available was the dim atmospheric lighting of the corridor that ran in front of the vaults.

I could vaguely make out a smaller room at the back of the vault near to where the spirit man Alexander was standing. I walked gingerly forward, carefully avoiding the stone circle in the centre of the room. I ignited my cigarette lighter in the hope of getting a glimmer of flame to light my way.

As I neared the area where the spirit man was standing, he suddenly disappeared, only to reappear a little further away from me.

I was now at the back of the vault. I could see the vague outline of Ray standing by the doorway.

As I stood there peering through the darkness, I felt a sudden blow to my chest. It was as though somebody had punched me very hard. I fell to my knees, feeling winded.

'Are you OK, Derek?' Ray shouted out. The fact that he had called me by my name and not the usual 'Ackers' told me that he was very much concerned, but I suspected that he assumed I had tripped over on the uneven floor.

'I'm OK, Ray,' I croaked as I got back to my feet, 'but don't come in – there's something in here.'

I saw a bright light in the doorway. Ray had flipped open his mobile phone to try and light the area a little. In that brief moment I saw clairvoyantly a number of men. They were standing around the outer perimeter of the stone circle.

Shuffling slowly, they began to move. Round and round they went. Clairaudiently I could hear chanting, but they were not praying to any god that I knew. This was dark energy. The men were praying to the dark forces. They were attempting to build up negative energy. This was black magic.

The men came to a halt. At the head of the circle, denoted by his air of officialdom, stood the spirit man I had seen when I first entered the vault. Again, the name 'Alexander' resounded in my head. I felt Sam draw close to me.

Alexander raised his arm and then brought it swiftly down. At that signal, a young man in his early twenties entered the circle. Unlike the others, he was not garbed in dark robes. In fact he was almost naked. He walked in what I can only describe as a dream-like state to the centre of the circle and stood there, head erect and eyes closed. Then he slowly dropped to his knees but the upper part of his body remained upright.

The leader of the hooded men reached with his right hand into the belt area of his robe and brought forth a long glistening knife that he raised slowly above his head. Was I about to witness the replay of a human sacrifice?

'Nooooo!' I shouted out.

'What's the matter, Derek?' I heard Ray's panicked voice asking.

'Stay back!' I shouted in reply. 'Stay where you are!'

I knew that Ray's presence in the doorway of the vault was my only chance of remaining grounded. If he entered the vault with me, we would both be in great danger, especially if in his panic to get to me he crossed the stone circle. It had to be just me and Sam against the powers of evil.

At that moment there came the sound of another shower of stones falling from the roof of the vault. To this day I do not know whether this was due to negative spiritual energy, whether it was the result of my loud shout or indeed whether it was something that naturally occurred within the vault itself. I am not a great believer in spirits throwing missiles. Experience has taught me that such 'phenomena' are more than likely to have a more physical explanation.

I felt a tremendous pressure bearing down on me. It felt as though a great weight was pressing down on my chest, even though I was not lying down but standing upright against the wall of the vault. I felt as though I could barely breathe. As I struggled to inhale, I heard a low evil chuckle. I felt as though I was about to lose consciousness, but I knew that I would have to summon the strength to beat this evil entity. I could not let him win. If I did, all would be lost. Sam was beside me, together with my legion of spiritual helpers. Ray was here for me in the physical world. I could overcome the horror of this evil entity Alexander.

I felt the area around me grow colder and colder. Icy fingers seemed to clutch at my throat and I was coughing and choking. I felt as though I was being lifted from my feet. As I gasped for breath, I prayed to my God for help and deliverance from this evil entity.

A sudden heat by my side told me that Sam was closer to my aura than he had ever been before. He was adding his prodigious spiritual strength to my weaker mortal spirit.

Slowly the grip on my throat relaxed and I slumped to the floor. The emanations of evil receded and faded. I heard a stumbling noise and saw the light of Ray's mobile phone illuminating his progress towards me across the vault. Some inner instinct, or perhaps Ray's own guardian angel, guided his steps towards me around the outer perimeter of the stone circle in the centre of the room. He was suddenly by my side, helping me to my feet.

'Derek! Derek! Come on, it's Ray. Come forward!' I heard his beloved voice with its comforting Liverpudlian accent and knew I was safe.

By the light of Ray's mobile phone we negotiated our way back to the doorway of the vault. Once more in the corridor, I related to Ray what had happened and told him about the implications of that stone circle.

'You know, the next time you have a bright idea like this, Ackers, count me out,' he said.

I was back to being 'Ackers' – so I knew that all was well!

CHAPTER FIVE

Hospital Trauma

I received a telephone call from the wife of a very dear friend. She sounded distressed. She told me that my friend John had been rushed into hospital earlier that morning and that he was seriously ill. I asked her for details of the hospital and the ward that he was on and told her that I would make my way there to see him.

I arrived at Walton Hospital some 45 minutes later. Upon my arrival I asked at reception for directions to the ward in which John was being treated, but I was told that I was in the wrong part of the building. I was re-routed to a different annexe and finally arrived at John's bedside.

I was shocked when I saw my dear friend. He was lying on a bed attached to all types of medical equipment and looked very poorly indeed. I leaned over and said quietly, 'Hi, John.'

He opened his eyes and smiled. 'Hello, stranger. I haven't seen you in a while,' he murmured to me through an oxygen mask. I had to lean close to him to hear his words.

He closed his eyes and seemed to drift off to sleep. I pulled up a chair and sat beside him, thinking about all the good times that we had shared together in the past. John was some years older than me, but we were of like mind and had similar interests. In short, we had enjoyed each other's company over the years of our friendship.

John's wife Mary and his two sons, Tony and Richie, arrived and drew up chairs next to the bed. John could not talk much and seemed to be drifting in and out of consciousness. Mary turned to me and asked worriedly, 'D'you think he'll be OK, Derek?'

It was not my place to voice my very real knowledge that John's time here in physical life was drawing to a close, so I merely nodded in response to her question. I knew that John would recover this time but it would not be many weeks before he would be back in the hospital for the last time. But I could not bring myself to burden his poor wife any further, as she was already beside herself with worry.

Richie was holding his father's hand when John suddenly told him, 'Don't worry, son, I'll be OK. I'll be on the mend and home soon.'

It was not long before John had recovered sufficiently to be released from hospital and I continued to visit him at his home. On one occasion he told me that his doctor and the specialist at the hospital had advised him that he required a triple bypass operation, and soon. He asked me, not just as his friend but as a medium, what I thought. I replied that if the doctors were telling him that he needed the operation, then he should take their advice and have it done.

At this time I had started demonstrating mediumship on stage in civic halls and small theatres. As a consequence I was travelling across the country and was away from home for much of the time. One night I was on my way home and decided to telephone John to see how he was getting on. Mary answered the telephone. She told me that John had undergone his bypass operation and had recovered well at first but then his recovery had slowed down. He was out of hospital now, but they both feared that it would not be long before he would need to go back there once more. I asked whether she felt it would be alright for me to visit him the following day and she told me that he would be glad to see me.

When I knocked on the door, it was John himself who opened it. I was shocked at the sight of him. He looked tired and drawn. In fact he looked very poorly indeed.

'I'm feeling knackered all the time and with all these bloody pills, I'm like a walking chemist's shop!' he laughed.

Mary made us a cup of tea and left for a visit to the shops. John and I had been talking for well over an hour when he began to tell me that he had been dreaming a lot over the last few nights about his mother, who had passed to spirit some years previously. He told me that he could remember vividly the whole content of his last dream.

'She looked so young, Derek. She talked to me, telling me that my dad was well too but that I couldn't see him yet. What d'you think she meant by "yet", Derek?'

I was very careful in my explanation. I sensed that John's mother was visiting him because of his illness. I also knew that John was more seriously ill than he imagined. Later, as I left to go home, I had a sense of not wanting to leave him.

That night I was woken by a load banging noise in the bedroom. The curtains were drawn, but a small amount of light from the street lighting illuminated the room dimly. I felt a touch on my forehead. I looked up and there stood a spirit woman whom I did not recognize.

She spoke to me gently. 'Derek, my son will be joining me and his father very soon. Do not upset yourself too much. The time is very close for him to leave his physical life. We know you understand the system of life.'

I knew that this was John's mother in spirit speaking to me. A moment later she was joined by a man who looked vaguely familiar. I realized that this was John's father, as they were both similar in colouring, size and facial features.

I jumped up out of bed and turned on the light. It was 3.45 a.m. I felt a desperate urge to telephone John's home immediately, but knew that it was out of the question. I couldn't sleep for the rest of the night.

When I felt that the time had arrived when I could make a telephone call I picked up the phone and dialled John's number.

Mary answered my call. 'Oh, Derek! John's been rushed into hospital – they took him in the early hours of this morning. I've just come back for a short while to collect some clean pyjamas for him. I know he'd like to see you, so will you come to the hospital now?'

I didn't need asking a second time. I jumped into my car and made my way to Walton.

When I arrived I could not go in to see John straight away as the nurses were with him dealing with some medical apparatus to which he was attached. After around 15 minutes I was allowed to see my friend. John was lying on a bed. He seemed virtually unconscious. I knew that his time to leave his physical life was close. I sat for an hour or more with my friend. I knew that this would be our last goodbye. I spoke to John gently, hoping that he could hear me, telling him that his mother and father had paid me a visit and that he should have no fear, just let go and take that wonderful journey into God's kingdom. I kissed his forehead and was about to leave.

Just as I was heading towards the door of the room, I was startled by the sudden manifestation of a man in spirit. I could see from the light surrounding him that he was highly evolved. He took John's right hand in his own and told me that he was the one of those who would have the pleasure and responsibility of taking John on his final journey to the 'spirit kingdom' very soon. I realized that this was John's spirit guide.

I had to leave the hospital to keep an appointment later in the day. When I arrived home during the course of the evening I telephoned John's home, but received no reply. I decided to telephone the hospital, only to be told that John had passed peacefully away during the late afternoon.

The following day Mary telephoned me. 'I know that John would like a last visit from you, Derek,' she said.

I could find no words to tell her that it would not be John she was asking me to visit, but the mere shell of John. The essence of the man, the part of him that I had grown so fond of over the years and had shared so much with, was now gone. Mary told me that John's body was lying in the hospital's chapel of rest. I agreed to go along to pay my respects.

As I looked down at John, lying there looking so peaceful, I thought of the pleasure that he would have felt when meeting up with his spirit family. John had been a devout believer in my work, so I knew that he would have no fear whatsoever in undertaking the transition from this life to the next.

After a few moments spent reflecting on the happy times we had spent together, I decided that it was time to go home. I made my way along the winding hospital corridors to the exit, which was two doors on swing hinges. Then I realized that somewhere along my journey I had taken a wrong turning and had ended up heading for the exit of the Accident & Emergency unit.

As I approached the doors, they flew open and all hell seemed to break loose. First one policeman, then two, together with what looked like a security man in uniform, charged through the doors. They held the doors open to allow a man in a wheelchair to be wheeled in. The man sitting in the chair was handcuffed and connected by a chain to yet another uniformed man. The policemen and security men were shouting for people to make way and let them through. Everyone sitting and standing around the area looked stunned.

As the man in the wheelchair was hurriedly pushed past me, he looked me directly in the eye. His expression held contempt and a certain amount of malice, but even more alarming was the spirit entity with him. This man seemed nothing less than pure evil. I knew right away that I was not meant to leave the hospital.

Sam materialized by my side. He told me that I was there for an added purpose – that I had been brought to the hospital not just to visit John's body but for the prisoner's sake as well.

At that moment a nurse approached me. 'Hello, Derek,' she said. 'What are you doing here?'

I told her about my friend and his sad passing.

'I know it's very rude of me to ask at a time like this,' she said, 'but if I get you a cup of tea, will you sign a few autographs for me and my friends? You can sit in this cubicle so you won't be interrupted.'

'How odd,' I thought to myself. I was often asked for autographs, but I had never been offered a cup of tea in exchange before. My only thought was that there must be a reason for it, especially in light of what Sam had had to say, so I agreed to the request.

The nurse showed me into a curtained-off area containing an empty bed and a chair, supplied me with a pen and some slips of paper and went off to get the promised cup of tea.

Whilst I was sitting there signing away, I heard voices coming through the curtain from the cubicle next door. A man's voice was asking, 'What happened?' I heard a gruff response talking about a fight and a stabbing. I realized it was the prisoner who had been rushed past me minutes earlier. He had obviously been rushed to hospital because he had been stabbed. This was confirmed when I heard another voice from the cubicle talking about the other prisoner having been hurt but not sufficiently for him to be brought out of prison.

Then I heard a raised voice, obviously the prisoner's, shouting, 'It was a fucking good thing you got me out then, because I was going to kill him!' This comment was followed by raucous laughter.

I turned around in my chair to look in the direction of the voice. As I did so, a hand reached out and pulled the curtain dividing the cubicles aside and I was face to face with the prisoner. As I looked, startled, into his eyes, I noticed that his face was beginning to change and transfigure. Suddenly I was looking at the evil spirit I had seen entering the hospital attached so closely to the prisoner. This man had to be helped – but how could I try to explain this to the police, the prison guards and the doctor? What a dilemma!

'And what are you doing there? What's wrong with you?' one of the policemen asked me brusquely.

I saw no point in trying to explain. I told them that I was leaving and, pulling back the curtain, stood up.

At that moment the nurse re-entered the cubicle, carrying my cup of tea. 'Are you going?' she asked.

I told her that I had better leave, passed her the signed slips of paper and went off to find the exit once more.

I stood outside the hospital and pondered what to do. I walked over to the car park and had a quiet cigarette whilst musing over the situation. How could I help anybody in these circumstances? Here was a prisoner who had attacked another and been stabbed but was still wanting to kill the other man.

'But Derek,' said Sam suddenly, 'you have missed a very important point! The man in the wheelchair does not truly wish to harm his fellow prisoner – it is the spirit who is with him who wishes the violence and evil.'

I realized that if something was not done then the evil entity would succeed and this would result in a killing. But I just did not know what to do.

Then I heard Sam's voice once more. He told me that the prisoner's injuries were not serious enough for surgery but that he would have to stay in the hospital overnight. He gave me a plan that would allow me to help him. He told me that the prisoner had been admitted to a room off the main A&E department. It was whilst he was locked in this room that I would have my opportunity to help. I was to lure the entity away from the prisoner. Once I had succeeded in doing this, Sam would ensure that he could not return to attach himself to the man once more. When this had been achieved, the entity would be dealt with outside the vicinity of the hospital.

I walked back into the hospital and went to the canteen to purchase a cup of coffee. This needed some thinking about. I wasn't at all sure about it. The last thing I wanted to do was to become involved in any way with the prisoner or the people who were escorting him. But Sam seemed to be pushing me into it.

After about an hour I returned to the A&E department. It was reasonably quiet at the time. I saw a room with a policeman standing outside and realized that this was the place where the prisoner would be spending the night. A doctor walked up to the policeman and spoke briefly to him. After ensuring that the door was securely locked, the policeman walked off with him in the direction of another room.

This was my opportunity! I walked quickly towards the door and tapped on it.

'Whaddaya want?' came a shout.

I said nothing out loud but silently began to goad the spirit entity. Although I had not said a word out loud, filthy and venomous words were then hurled in my direction. I felt a huge rush of energy envelop me and felt the features of my face alter. It was with a tremendous effort that I backed away from the door. As I did so, I heard a weak voice saying, 'Thank you. Whoever you are, thank you!'

I heard footsteps coming back along the corridor and quickly turned and hurried around a corner. When I glanced back, I realized that I had been just in time to avoid being caught by the policeman, who was now taking up his position again in front of the prisoner's door.

I felt terrible. I was desperately attempting to keep a grip on reality whilst inwardly wrestling with the vicious and evil spirit entity which I had lured away from the hapless prisoner. I went outside and reached the now dark car park. I could hear a voice in my head raving and cursing and I felt as though my limbs were jerking uncontrollably.

'Take this away from me, Sam!' I shouted. 'I can't stand it!'

I managed to stagger to a quiet spot at the side of the car park where there was a small garden containing a bench. I sat down on the bench and focused all my energy on helping Sam eject the spirit entity from my aura. I could hear Sam's voice talking and reasoning with quiet persuasion. Gradually, I felt warmth and light enveloping me. My arms and legs relaxed and I felt the muscles in my face return to normal. Sam had dispatched the entity to his designated realm. He would bother nobody again.

I heard Sam's voice talking to me once more. He told me that in his lifetime the spirit man had committed a double murder. He had received a life sentence but had decided that rather than spend the rest of his physical time on Earth in prison he would take himself over by committing suicide. He had succeeded in doing this by hanging himself in his prison cell. His spirit had remained in that cell until its new occupant arrived – the man who had been admitted to hospital. He too had committed murder and he too had been given a life sentence. The man in spirit had attached himself to him and had remained with him, causing untold trouble. One wretched soul is bad enough, but two create constant mayhem. This demonstrated to me perfectly that 'like attracts like'.

Wearily, I climbed into my car. Feeling in need of some peace, I took a drive towards Crosby Marina. The moonlight played on the waters of the river Mersey and I could hear the waves lapping against the sandy shore.

As I looked towards the water I saw two spirit figures – one was a monk and the other a very serene-looking lady. I heard a quiet voice saying, 'Thank you for helping Arthur.'

I was puzzled, then I realized that Arthur was the prisoner who had been admitted to hospital.

It matters not what crimes we commit during our stay here on this physical Earth, we still have our guides and we still have people who care for us. We all have to atone for our misdeeds, but when this has been achieved, our loved ones are still there waiting for us.

About to close the window to my car, I looked once more towards the sands where I had seen the two figures. There was nothing there, but a moment later I noticed another light dancing and gradually growing. Within a moment or two, there stood the spirit of my dear friend John. He looked at me and smiled. Then he saluted me goodbye and he was gone.

CHAPTER SIX

Carnage in California

In 1999 I took my first trip to Hollywood, California, to join a group of paranormal investigators who had been established in Los Angeles since the mid-nineties. I had been asked to undertake this trip by my then manager, who thought it might be good for my career to undertake psychic investigations not only in the UK but in the USA as well. I was not sure what I was letting myself in for, but I was assured that the group was serious in its investigative methods. It was to be the first time that I had ever been involved in investigations of allegedly haunted sites using EMF meters, temperature gauges and other items of 'ghost detection' equipment. Prior to this, any investigations in which I had been involved had merely consisted of me opening myself up to the atmosphere and any spiritual vibrations present and explaining what I picked up. The only measurement of cold spots and hot spots was what I and anyone who happened to be with me noticed. This was going to be an interesting experiment!

We arrived at LAX airport in the middle of the afternoon Los Angeles time. I was concerned to discover that after a wash and brush up I would be taken to meet the rest of the group I would be working with, which consisted of the well-known American medium Peter James together with two 'empathics', a term used to describe people who are sensitive to atmospheres but who neither see nor hear spirits, a parapsychologist and two people who would be taking care of the technical equipment and hand-held camera. Although these people all appeared to be very nice and sincere, it was not the sort of situation I was used to working in. Added to this, I was seriously jet lagged, having been out of my bed since four in the morning UK time and taken an 11-hour flight, and my body was of course telling me that although it might be early evening in California, it was the middle of the night at home and I should be tucked up in bed asleep. I was grateful when the time came for us to retire to bed, because the following day I was expected to take part in a full-scale investigation of not one but two locations in the Hollywood area.

At 9 o'clock the following morning my manager, his wife, my own wife Gwen and I were collected from the hotel by the parapsychologist and his assistant. They told us that they were taking us to a house in the Hollywood Hills known as Cresthill Mansion. I knew nothing about this property but was confident that I could do the investigation justice.

On arriving at the house I was surprised to see outside broadcast trucks parked in the road and a plethora of reporters holding microphones. They were obviously from local radio, television and newspapers, who had been alerted to the fact that a ghost investigation was about to take place.

After a number of interviews in which I was asked to explain what I expected to find in the house, the time came for us to walk through the front door.

The house itself was what I would describe as Spanish in style, with walls colourwashed a bright pink. It had an enormous studded front door. Although at one time it had resounded with the noise of late-night partying, now the interior lay empty and was eerily quiet. The footsteps of the team sounded on the bare floorboards as we made our way from room to room.

I gradually opened up my psychic senses to the residual energies of the house – those energies absorbed by the fabric of the building. I sensed that at one time it had been a centre of opulence and money – lots of money spent on self-indulgence. I quietly asked Sam why on Earth I would be brought to such a place if there was nothing more than past energy and memories to report. 'You'll see!' came his mysterious reply.

As the moments passed, a picture began to build in my mind. This had not always been a happy household. It had been well known and feared for what went on within its walls. I received a mental image of violence and intrigue, one man against another, and people afraid to speak out for fear of recrimination.

As I mounted the stairs with Peter James, he suddenly shouted, 'Samuel!'

Startled, I looked in the direction in which he was pointing. I was horrified to see clairvoyantly a pool of blood forming on the small square half-landing. It grew and grew and began to run and drip over the edge of the open galleried stairway and down onto the floor of the hallway below.

Almost immediately I felt a sharp but terrible pain in my temple. I had to make a tremendous effort to stop myself from clutching my head and falling to the floor.

'Have no fear, Derek,' I heard Sam tell me. 'You are safe!'

Slowly the pain began to recede. I knew that what I had just experienced, for the first time in my life, was the physical effect of a gunshot wound to my head. I looked down at my feet and saw the vague outline of a man's body lying on the stairway. It was obvious that what I was experiencing was the action replay of a shooting.

I shakily descended the stairs and followed the rest of the group to the kitchen area. Here I picked up the sensation of fear once more, of a callous disregard for life, of a mind-set where people were as expendable as a used coffee cup. The whole house reverberated with a false and empty joyousness with an underlying element of fear – people afraid of doing the wrong thing or speaking to the wrong people.

We progressed to another room where there was a trap door in the floor. The parapsychologist opened it up. 'What d'you think, Derek?' he asked me.

I gingerly descended the few steps and was met by a blank wall. I gained the distinct impression that this was an escape route – a way to somewhere that was now blocked up for all time. It had something to do with another property close by, of that I was sure.

We continued our investigation, roving from room to room and gazing in awe at the marbled bathrooms with their solid gold fittings. All through the house the same emotions prevailed – fear and desolation under an outward veneer of happiness, partying and joy.

At the end of the investigation I was informed that the house had once been owned by the Mafia. Call girls were often brought there for the entertainment of the gang members. Such women were worthless and expendable. People could also pay the ultimate price for a loose tongue and that was the story of the man on the stairs.

I was glad that I had picked up no actual spirit presence in the house. I would have been saddened indeed to discover that any person seeing their life end there had felt drawn back to it for any reason. At lease I could be happy in the knowledge that the people who had passed to the spirit world from those premises were at peace and dwelling in serenity in the world of spirit. They had not been bad people – they had not been gang members themselves but mere pawns used in the terrible times when gang warfare was at its height.

I was more than a little shaken by what I had experienced at Cresthill Mansion. Looking at this pleasant home in the Hollywood Hills, nobody would ever guess that it had played host to the events I had witnessed clairvoyantly during the investigation. Knowing that there was another investigation to come, I was concerned that the house had drained me psychically.

After a lunch break at a diner on Sunset Boulevard we moved on to the next location. This was a large square building painted black. The name 'Comedy Store' was affixed to it in large stainless steel lettering. The team gathered together and in we went.

We walked along a corridor with large black-and-white framed photographs of modern American comedians hanging on the walls and came to a large room full of tables and chairs and with black patent leather upholstered bench seating affixed to the wall. At the front of the room there was a semi-circular stage raised about 18 inches above the level of the floor. The whole room was amazing. It was like taking a step back in time to the days of art deco.

Immediately I entered the room, followed by the rest of the team, I clairaudiently heard the name 'Suzanne' whispered in my ear. As I watched, the spirit form of a young woman built up before me. She seemed to be beckoning the whole team in and making gestures of welcome.

After a few moments she was joined by the spirit form of a small stocky man. He was dapper in dress and I had the distinct impression that he had been involved in music – maybe he had played the piano at the club, because as I watched he went through the motions of running his fingers up and down the keyboard of a piano that was standing to the side of the stage. Although this man seemed cheerful enough in his appearance I knew that there was an underlying sadness with him. His spirit was in visitation, reliving the fact that he had lost the love of his life – his wife. I had little time to wonder why he was not together with her in the world of spirit. I knew that during his life-time he had suffered with his health and had under-gone surgery, but I was unsure whether he had passed over to the spirit world as a result of it. I was impressed with the name 'Francis'.

In the darkness of the room I could make out the spirit forms of many people who had once visited the nightclub. They came and went, faded and appeared again in other parts of the room. Francis also continued flitting around. It was obvious that he had been used to people visiting his old workplace and no doubt took joy in reliving his old career night after night and being part of the party atmosphere, just as he had when he had been part of the physical life of the club.

As more and more spirit people came and went, the temperature of the club began to drop dramatically and this was recorded on the temperature meter held by one of the team.

We moved on deeper into the club and all the time our senses were assailed by the presence of the spirit people. It was obvious to me that the history of the building stretched much further back than the modern-day Comedy Store.

We climbed a further set of stairs and entered yet another room. Much as in the main salon, this room contained tables and the art deco style of furnishings was evident once more. The atmosphere, however, had altered drastically. Gone was the feeling of fun and bonhomie prevalent in the downstairs area. Here there was a far more sinister, heavy-laden air.

I knew almost immediately that suffering and death had taken place within these walls. I could hear screaming and smell the stench of blood. My head was pounding with the pressure of emotion. I could hear babies crying, but these were the cries of children not born to this Earth but rather whose gestation had been suddenly and forcefully brought to a halt by the intervention of doctors paid to abort.

'Stop the cameras!' I shouted. I was having great difficulty in coming to terms with the wholesale destruction of so many brief lives. I could also sense the physical and emotional agony suffered by the young women who had been forced to undergo these barbaric operations. The whole of my body seemed agonized to a point where I felt almost faint. I experienced a great longing for life – a knowledge that I was about to pass on to the spirit world but that I did not want to.

'Take it off, Sam,' I pleaded, praying to be released from the agony I was experiencing. I managed to gain a hold once more on my senses so that we could continue the investigation.

We continued on, walking through the meandering halls and rooms of the old club. I sensed Mafia connections, deals done and deals broken, lives lost violently. I heard shouting and gunshots. Francis was still flitting in and out and I knew that he had been heavily involved in the side of the club that people did not see. The Comedy Store was indeed a place to see and be seen in the days gone by, but it was also a place to fear if you knew too much or were involved with the wrong people.

At the end of the investigation I was told that the Comedy Store had started life in 1939 as Ciro's, a well-known Hollywood nightclub. This was a place where movie stars loved to be seen in the post-World War II years. It was not unusual for the late great Frank Sinatra to be seen visiting the club, but sadly, on the occasion of my visit, his spirit did not choose to make itself known.

The night spot's popularity waned in the sixties and it eventually came into the ownership of Mitzi Shore, mother of the comedian Pauly Shore. Mitzi was at that time also the owner of Cresthill Mansion, the location of the previous investigation. How strange that the house and the club should have such historical ties.

CHAPTER SEVEN

A Moment's Madness

I was in the middle of my theatre tour around the UK. Ray and I had travelled the country in the preceding weeks but knew that we had many more miles to go before we could look forward to a break.

We reached the county of Cambridgeshire and drove to the town where I would be appearing at the local theatre that night. After unpacking my bags once again and having a meal, I eventually arrived at the theatre around 6 p.m. The show, as usual, was successful.

At the end of every show it is my practice to go to the front of the theatre to meet people who have attended and, if they should require it, sign autographs and have photographs taken with them. This particular night the queue snaked around the foyer of the theatre. I shook hands and signed autographs for each person as they approached the table at which I was sitting.

All the time I was doing this I was aware of a couple who were standing not too far away from me. They were not in the queue and seemed to keep glancing nervously at me. They were so close to me that I could feel their nervousness washing over me. It was most disquieting and it was drawing my attention away from the people who had queued up to meet me. I beckoned to Ray and asked him why the two people were standing there and not queuing up.

'Don't know, Ackers,' he said. 'Perhaps they're here to see me!' He laughed. 'I'll keep an eye on them, though.'

Ray then approached the couple to ask them if they were waiting to see me. They told him that they wanted to ask me a question about something that was bothering them. Ray asked them to join the end of the queue. 'Derek will speak to you then,' he told them.

It was after midnight before I actually got to speak to the two people, who introduced themselves as Mike and Jenny. Their question related to their home. They had moved in some two years earlier and it had been a dream come true for them. They had not thought that they would ever be able to buy a home of their own, but a small cottage in a village a few miles away from where they were living had come onto the market at a remarkably low price. Suspecting that there might be some major problems with the building, they had commissioned a complete structural engineer's survey, but nothing untoward had been brought to light. Joyfully, Mike and Jenny had paid over the deposit, completed the purchase process and moved in.

It was only then that they realized why the asking price had been so low. From almost the moment they moved into their dream home they began to experience strange goings-on. Items in the house would move inexplicably, there would be strange groaning noises and what sounded like a suffering child crying out in agony. These noises could be experienced at any time. Also, the atmosphere of the cottage, they told me, sometimes seemed to be so heavy with depression that they were beginning to feel depressed all the time themselves and it had got to the point where they dreaded going home after work.

'Please could you come to see the place for yourself, Derek?' they asked me. 'We can't pay you, but we really are desperate!'

I could see that this couple were at the end of their tether and I felt that I had to help them. Fortunately, apart from a book signing at lunchtime the next day, I was free before travelling on to the next theatre booking. I told the couple that I did not make a charge for my services away from theatre and television work, so money was not an issue, and said that I would be prepared to visit their home early the following evening if that was convenient for them. Relieved, they readily agreed.

The following day at around 5.30 p.m. Ray and I made our way to Mike and Jenny's house. Their cottage was the second in a row of pleasant-looking small houses on a quiet road.

Ray parked the car. We walked up the path and knocked on the door. Mike answered almost immediately.

The front door opened onto a living area; there was no hallway. Mike took us through this area into the kitchen beyond. The stairs to the upper floor led straight up out of the kitchen. The house was in fact a small but quaint Victorian worker's cottage.

On entering the house I had detected no spirit presence. It was not long, however, before I saw a woman in spirit hovering near the bottom of the staircase. She was remarkably good looking and, although obviously of working stock, was neat and clean in appearance. She had an almost haughty air about her.

Slowly the spirit form of a man built up as well. He too looked well turned out and sober in appearance.

What I did not understand about this very respectable-looking spirit couple was the air of complete sadness and depression that seemed to surround them and enshroud the atmosphere as soon as they appeared. I sensed no danger with them and indeed, although I knew that Sam was close by, sensed no urgency with him and heard no warning from him. There was no risk here, just an innate and deep-seated sadness. There was something terrible tying this couple, the woman especially, to this house.

'Edward has progressed,' I heard Sam's voice telling me, 'but Ann refuses to leave. She cannot forgive herself for what she did and does not see how she can receive forgiveness in the world of spirit.'

These words told me that the problems Mike and Jenny were experiencing were directly attached to Ann's spiritual presence in their home. It was her guilt that was the cause of the feelings of depression and unrest within the cottage. But what was the reason for it?

Sam supplied the answer. 'Ann always wanted more out of life than Edward could give her,' he told me. 'She wanted material possessions – she became obsessed with wanting to be better than the people around her.'

Psychically, I had the feeling that the upper floor of the house was the least affected. I was sure that the room at the front of the house would hold the answer to my question. I asked Mike whether I could go back into the living-room area. He led me through.

Back in the living room, I opened myself up completely to its emanations and atmosphere. A home came to my mind, a comfortable home, as this cottage had been in the days when Ann and Edward had occupied it. Nevertheless I picked up a feeling of dissatisfaction with the woman – a feeling of this not being enough, a wish for better things.

'Sanderson, Sanderson, Sanderson!' This name played through my mind. Was this the surname of the family?

With Edward I picked up a feeling of desertion – of him sitting alone with his head in his hands and then experiencing a joyous homecoming. There were children too – five of them! There was joy with the man and his children, but still utter sadness and dissatisfaction with the woman.

As I stood there, the atmosphere in the room became heavy and deep. I saw the five children lying on the floor – all gone. All had passed to the spirit world. Ann stood over them with her hands to her face, then she too fell to the floor. Gone! All of them!

The air around me swirled with the deepest depression I have ever felt in my life. Tears sprung to my eyes and I felt my shoulders heave with grief. The word 'arsenic' flew into my mind. Then all was silent.

Ray, Mike and Jenny were standing silently, hardly daring to breathe. 'Are you OK, Derek?' I heard Ray ask. I merely nodded. I was so desperately sad, I was unable to speak.

Sam spoke again. 'She poisoned herself and her children with arsenic,' he said. 'She was unhappy with her lot. Now she is determined that the unhappiness and depression that she suffered will be experienced by anybody who occupies this home.'

The images played out before my clairvoyant eye were as desperate as anything I had ever experienced.

Here was a situation where a woman was so unhappy in life that she had decided to take herself and her children over to the world of spirit. She had given no thought to the fact that she was robbing her five children of what could have been a happy and fulfilled physical life here on Earth. She had given no thought to anything other than herself and her dissatisfaction and her greed – her wish for 'one-upmanship'.

I was amazed by the fact that in spite of what she had done, her husband could forgive her. Indeed, he was unwilling to leave her and had repeatedly returned from his home in the heavenly state with his children to the place where his wife's spirit still remained and where she had seen an end to what she thought of as her hell on Earth.

During my time as an investigative medium I had come into contact with many spirit people with many diverse personality traits. I had met evil spirits who had been determined to cause me harm, I had battled with entities who had carried out horrendous deeds against their fellow men during their time on this physical plane, but I had never met any person, either alive or in spirit, with the willpower of the spirit woman who stood before me.

The spirit of Edward once more built up in front of me. 'Help her, Derek,' he pleaded. 'Please help me to help her.'

I had no choice.

I started by speaking out into the atmosphere to Ann. I told her that she could not continue as she was. She would have to move on to the world of spirit properly. Her children and her husband had forgiven her. They understood that although what she had done was a terrible thing, it was a moment of madness that had overtaken her. I called upon her children – Eleanor, James, Margaret, Robert and William – to join their father Edward and add their voices to his in calling to their mother. I asked Sam and all my guardians and helpers to add their not inconsiderable spirit energy in sending Ann to the light where she would quickly progress to a place where she could dwell in the heavenly state with her family. I told her that never had a woman been loved so much but never had a woman been so unaware of that fact. I prayed hard to my God to intervene.

Slowly the atmosphere in the room lightened. A huge weight seemed to lift. A smattering of spirit lights twinkled and rained down in the centre of the room.

There was a feeling of being able to breathe freely. I felt the beginnings of laughter and chuckled out loud. I looked round to Ray, Mike and Jenny and saw that they were smiling too. Their own psychic senses were telling them that whatever had been in the home was now gone, never to return.

I told Mike and Jenny about the woman and her husband and children.

'When did all this happen, Derek?' Mike asked.

'A long time ago – maybe 150 years or so,' I told him.

'Poor woman,' Jenny remarked. 'She must have been suffering terribly to do such a thing.'

I agreed, but there was something that I cannot and will never understand. Some people are dissatisfied with their lot in life. They have so much, but they still want more. So many terrible things are all down to that one small word and huge emotion – greed!

CHAPTER EIGHT

The Murderous Monk

Ormskirk and the surrounding areas hold many memories of the English Civil War. At the time there was much activity in the region. Lathom House withstood a prolonged Parliamentary assault before it surrendered in 1645, after which there was an order for it to be destroyed, and ever since that time there have been reports of people hearing the sounds of battle on the site – gunshots and the sound of men screaming and shouting. The ghostly forms of Parliamentary soldiers and cavaliers have also been seen in the area, only to disappear just as suddenly as they appeared.

Nearby is the village of Burscough, which lies close to Martin Mere – at one time one of the largest lakes in

England. Basket-making was a primary industry here. It was also home to the monks of Burscough Priory.

Deep in this part of Lancashire there is also a large country house. I am unable to name it, because it is a private dwelling and I would not wish to compromise the privacy of the owners. The house itself has a long and colourful history and is old enough to have seen the rivalries of the English Civil War when Cromwell strode with his armies through this tranquil part of the country.

The owners of this old Lancashire manor house wrote to tell me that they were having a problem and asked whether I would come along to investigate. At the time I had closed my office in Liverpool and no longer conducted personal sittings on a regular basis. I had been working in television for quite some time and travelling up and down the country appearing in various theatres throughout the UK and the Republic of Ireland. People could no longer contact me by telephone, but I received, and still do receive, a huge mailbag, which included this letter. The couple had given me their telephone number and I was intrigued enough to arrange a meeting at their home.

* * *

Peter and Lucy are in their mid-forties. They had owned their house for almost 15 years, having bought it in quite a derelict state and sunk a huge amount of money and time into the renovation of the old building.

When I arrived, I was absolutely amazed at the beauty and size of the building. It was constructed of a soft buttery-coloured sandstone. The front of the house had numerous windows peeping out from the foliage of an enormous wisteria that was still clinging on to its late autumn leaves. In front of the house was laid a circular neatly clipped lawn, in the centre of which stood an enormous and ancient-looking oak tree. All of this was surrounded by a gravel driveway.

I had not expected such grandeur, but if I was amazed by the exterior of the building, it was nothing to my surprise as I stepped through the front door. The hallway was enormous and galleried, with a black-and-white marble-tiled floor. Two staircases carpeted in rich red swept up on either side to the gallery above, while corridors to the left and the right led off to good-ness knows where in the depths of the house.

'You look surprised,' Lucy said to me as she led me down one of these corridors and through a door which opened onto a comfortable sitting room. A fire blazed in the enormous grate.

'Do sit down.' Lucy gestured towards a deep and comfortable leather sofa. She then proceeded to tell me how hard she and Peter had worked to achieve such a beautiful home and how much they had had to forgo to be able to restore the house. They had been determined that everything would be done properly – that they would not stint by using cheap methods of refurbishment but would make sure that when they were finished, the house would be returned to its former glory. They had certainly achieved their aim.

Lucy apologized for the fact that Peter had been called away to work suddenly. 'He shouldn't be too long though,' she added.

She explained that she and Peter had always known that the house was 'haunted', as she termed it, because they had both experienced odd little things happening – items being moved inexplicably and glimpses of somebody or something around the corridors or on the stairs. Just lately, though, as they had come to the end of all the building work, things had begun to feel more sinister. Lucy said she couldn't explain exactly what she meant, but she was sure I would understand when I had walked around the house myself.

In the meantime she excused herself for a few minutes to make me a cup of tea. Whilst I was in the room on my own, I took the opportunity to open myself up to the emanations of the house.

As soon as I had entered the front door I had been aware that there was indeed spirit activity in the house, but I had not picked up anything of a malevolent nature. As I sat in the fire-warmed sitting room I was even more aware of activity – particularly of a young woman who I knew would roam the house, going from room to room, revisiting the places she had loved when she herself had once lived there. I was also aware that children from the spirit world would visit the old house from time to time and play in the rooms and corridors. Again, though, I could sense nothing that would lead me to think that they had upset the atmosphere of the home. All in all, I couldn't pick up anything that would create a problem. In fact, if anything, I would say that the feelings I was receiving at that time were calm, peaceful and warm.

When Lucy returned with the tea, I told her that I had been sitting there absorbing the emanations of the house but could feel nothing untoward – nothing other than peace and calm.

'When you've finished your tea, Derek, I'll take you on a tour of the house to see what you think,' she told me.

Some 15 minutes later Lucy took me on a conducted tour of the manor house. I really do not know how she remembered which corridors led where, but as we progressed towards the other end of the house I began to feel the atmosphere changing. We reached a point where there was a dramatic change in that it became colder, damper and not nearly so pleasant. As Lucy led me into each room in turn I began feeling more uncomfortable and uneasy. I asked her whether she noticed any difference between this part of her house and the earlier part, and she told me that she did not feel nearly so comfortable sitting in the rooms in this area as she did in the first sitting room she had taken me into. The atmosphere certainly had nothing to do with the furnishings, as this part of the house had been just as grandly refurbished and decorated as the other part.

We continued on. The same sensation overcame me as we progressed through the upper floor of the house – we came to a point where the atmosphere changed from being warm and comfortable to being cold and damp and not nearly so appealing. I had never ever felt such a definition of atmospheres.

Lucy was about to solve the problem, though. She told me that the first part of the house – the part in which we had enjoyed our tea – was the original building. It had been standing on the land for some 800 years, whilst the second part of the building – the part where I detected a great divide in atmospheres – had been built some 300 years later, using stones and timbers transported from another large country house.

We arrived back on the ground floor with just one or two smaller rooms to visit.

'What is this room?' I asked Lucy, pointing to a doorway to which I felt particularly drawn.

'Oh, that's nothing,' she told me. 'It's a doorway to nowhere! And the other room is a guest bathroom.'

I opened the 'doorway to nowhere' and found that it was in fact a narrow cupboard. I stood inside the small area and became immediately aware of the spirit form of a boy.

'Thomas's son,' Sam whispered to me.

The spirit boy seemed unconcerned at my presence but quickly faded away. I knew that he was one of the children whose presence I had sensed earlier. Sam was not forthcoming with any more information on the boy or any of the other children.

I stepped out and closed the cupboard.

Lucy opened the door to the guest bathroom and I could see a large room with a hand basin and toilet, but what I could also see was the figure of a man. He was wearing a dark monk's habit with the hood drawn down over his face. I immediately sensed that this spirit entity was the cause of the problems. I walked towards him. As I did so, I could sense anger and hostility. As I drew nearer, he appeared almost to jump away from me. As I entered the area of the room where he had previously been standing, I could pick up a cold and dank atmosphere. I almost felt as though I had walked into a deep pool of cold, stagnant and evil-smelling water.

'I really dislike this room and will never go into it on my own,' Lucy told me. 'Many people who have visited the house have said exactly the same thing. And as for the smell! No matter what we do, it won't go away. We've had the drains checked and there's nothing whatsoever wrong with them. We really don't know what the problem is.'

I told Lucy that I had seen a tall male figure dressed in a monk's habit in the room and that he did not have the usual calm and peaceful emanations of a man of the cloth but had a more evil air about him.

At that point we both heard footsteps on the stairs. We were joined by a tall athletic-looking gentleman. Lucy introduced him as her husband Peter.

'Have you found anything yet, Derek?' he asked me.

I repeated what I had said to Lucy.

'Ah!' he said. 'I'm not surprised, because this part of the house was built with materials taken from a monastery that was destroyed. Could it be that this fellow has followed the bits and pieces of his old home? In fact in the grounds there are the ruins of a small chapel. We call it "the Monk's Walk", because there is a story around these parts that monks have been seen in the area walking around. Would you like to see it?'

I readily agreed.

By this time it was late afternoon and the daylight was beginning to fade rapidly. Armed with torches, Peter and I set out across the fields, heading in the direction of a distant clump of trees.

As we neared the trees I could vaguely make out the outline of the ruins of a comparatively small building. As we drew closer still, I could see the marks on the remaining walls where burning torches had once been placed. There was an old, by now weather-beaten stone altar, and as I scraped back the fallen leaves, I could make out an uneven flagged floor beneath our feet. Vines and creepers had rambled over much of the lower stonework, but it was plain that this had once been a place of prayer.

Peter shuddered as a blast of cold air blew around us. 'The wind's got up,' he observed.

I knew, however, that this was not windy weather. The strong gust of air indicated to me that we had been joined by the tall man I had seen in the bath-room at the house. Once again he was swathed in the long hooded monk-like habit. Once again the emana-tions surrounding him bore no resemblance to the peace and calm I would normally expect to detect in an area such as this or surrounding a person who had, during their lifetime on this physical plane, lived by the word of God. This was no monk! This was some-body dressing in religious garb in order to hurt and confuse.

I felt Sam draw close to me. I knew that my guardians and keepers were surrounding me with protection.

'This man was a bad person when he was in his physical life,' Sam told me. 'He masqueraded as a monk to lure people into trusting him. Many a person has been lulled by his quiet and priestly words, only to find themselves held at knifepoint and robbed. This man has killed many times. He has violated women and harmed children. He is indeed an evil soul. Take great care, Derek. He will think nothing of trying to cause you harm.'

I was horrified. I knew that I could be in mortal danger, but I also knew that I had to do something to help Lucy and Peter reclaim their lovely home from what could be a potentially nightmare existence. They had done nothing to evoke this callous spirit – he was merely laying claim to an area he looked upon as his. If I did not help them, I knew that he would take a greater hold and his presence would become more pronounced. The cold and evil emanations would gradually spread throughout the whole building.

As I stood there staring at the dark sinister figure, I was more than relieved to know that Sam and the people from the spirit world who act as guardians to me were in close attendance.

As the dark figure stood by the ruins of the chapel, I saw movement to the left and the right of him and heard Sam utter what I can only describe as a sigh of relief. The figures of two men slowly evolved before my eyes. The power of goodness flowed from them.

'Bernard and Jude,' I heard Sam murmur. 'Highly evolved souls.'

'Bernard and Jude?' I repeated.

Peter broke in, asking, 'Did you mention the name "Bernard"?'

I nodded in reply.

'Bernard was a priest I remember from my childhood,' Peter told me. 'He was the most lovely and loving man. He taught at my school. I always remember him being so kind and caring. If ever I had a problem it was to Father Bernard that I took it. He was quite old when he died some 20 years ago.'

Sam explained to me that Bernard and Jude, both monks when they lived on this physical plane, had come to help me. With their help and that of Sam and my other guides and gatekeepers, I had to lure the evil-spirited man towards a vortex* or spiritual gate-way. Once I had led him to it, they would use their collective powers to force him to relinquish his hold on the area and to pass through the vortex into the spirit world proper, where he would be taken to a place of learning to atone for his actions during his time here on Earth. No more would he prowl the corridors of the house, no more would he roam the gardens and the beautiful walkways, no more would he infect the area with his evil emanations.

But how to do what was required of me? How could I, a mere mortal, achieve what Sam was expecting of me?

'It's going to be difficult, Derek,' he told me, 'but with our help you can do it.'

I moved carefully around the area. What with the fail-ing light and the dense undergrowth, the conditions underfoot were difficult. Ivy had grown across the pathway, presenting a hazard at every step. The ground

---

* A vortex is a portal or doorway in the atmosphere where spirit people enter or exit our physical world. Wherever there is spirit activity, there will always be a vortex. They are usually detectable by a sudden drop in temper-ature in a particular area. They do not move about, but remain static.

was wet and the remains of the tiled floor of the chapel glistened in Peter's torchlight.

As I drew closer to the place where the altar had once stood I felt the temperature drop dramatically. I had found the vortex! All I had to do now was draw the evil spirit man towards that area. I wondered whether he was aware of the plan, but as I looked towards him as he stood at the edge of what would have been the chapel wall, I doubted it. He seemed intent on watching my every move, waiting for me to slip and fall – waiting for me to harm myself.

I could see a slight movement out of the corner of my eye and knew that Sam had joined Bernard and Jude and all three were standing alongside me at the point of the vortex near the altar. The evil entity did not seem aware of their presence – perhaps they were too highly evolved – but I knew that he was now aware of the spiritual gateway and he was determined not to go near it. He did not want to move on from the place he considered to be his.

The only way Sam's plan could be achieved would be for me to get closer to the spirit man – close enough to make him forget his fear in his desire to try to harm me.

I carefully edged forward, closer and closer to the dark spirit. I could feel the emanations of evil leaping from him. Still I edged forward. The air almost crackled with the hatred he was throwing out towards me.

'Come on!' I challenged him.

All this time Peter had been standing shining his torch in my direction, but he was unaware of the drama that was unfolding. 'Who are you talking to, Derek?' he shouted.

'Don't worry, Peter. Just keep shining the torch on the ground at my feet,' I replied.

Seizing the opportunity provided by this momentary diversion, the evil spirit made a darting movement towards me. I leaped back, praying that I would keep my footing.

He made another move and another. On each occasion I moved back quickly, making sure that my moves brought us both nearer and nearer to the altar area where Sam, Bernard and Judge were waiting to help me.

Two more lunges forward by the spirit man and two hasty retreats on my part brought us both within a yard or two of the vortex. I had almost achieved my aim.

'You can't hurt me, you evil person!' I told him

levelly. 'You can't ever hurt anyone. You are no longer of this Earth! This does not belong to you!'

At that he threw himself towards me, determined to harm me in some way. I stepped back rapidly. As I did so, my foot caught in the rambling ivy covering the ground. I went down and hit the ground heavily, feeling a moment of real fear.

I needn't have worried, however. As I landed, I felt an enormous rush of cold air. I had managed to get this evil entity to the area where Sam and the two monks were waiting to bundle him through to the astral plane and send him on his way to finally begin to earn his place in the world of spirit.

I heard the frantic thud of feet running towards me. The footsteps slowed as Peter carefully negotiated the tangle of vine roots and creeping ivy.

'Are you alright, Derek?' he panted, as he arrived at the place where I was lying, winded by my fall.

'I'm OK, Peter,' I told him as I got painfully to my feet. 'And I don't think you'll have any more problems now.'

I sent out a silent prayer of thanks to Sam and his two helpers.

'And thank you too, Derek,' I heard a voice say. I knew that it was Bernard's voice.

As Peter and I walked back to the house I told him what had happened. 'I knew something was going on,' he said, 'because I could hear you jabbering away to yourself and then just as you fell there was a tremendous gust of wind just by where the old altar used to stand, and then there was silence and complete quiet. You could have almost heard a pin drop, it felt so utterly peaceful. I've never experienced that feeling at the chapel ruins before. You would expect anywhere that had once been a house of God to be a lovely calm area, but I've always done my best to avoid that chapel because it felt so horrible. The dogs weren't at all keen on going there either. Perhaps things will change now.'

'Indeed they will,' I told him.

Some weeks later the telephone rang at my house. It was Lucy.

'I'd like to thank you, Derek,' she said, 'for giving us back our home. Since your visit everything has been so much better. The house feels like ours now. Whereas once we thought that we might have to sell it, now we wouldn't part with it because it feels for the first time that it is truly our home.'

CHAPTER NINE

Bewitched

My visit to the Kirkstone Pass Inn happened quite by accident one warm September Sunday. Because the weather was so beautiful and unseasonably warm, and because for once we had some time off together, Gwen and I had travelled to Windermere to take lunch in the beautiful Cumbrian countryside. We had spent a few hours ambling around and had eaten well in one of the numerous eating establishments around Lake Windermere, and it was late afternoon when we decided to start a leisurely drive home.

I do not have the best sense of direction and managed to take a wrong turning out of Windermere town, which meant that we were travelling in the opposite direction to that which we should have taken. As we drove along looking for somewhere to turn round on the narrow road, Gwen noticed a sign: 'Kirkstone Pass'.

'I've heard so much about a pub called the Kirkstone Pass Inn,' she said. 'I'd love to visit it to see if you can pick up anything from the energies there. It's supposed to be very haunted.'

I don't usually like to work in my precious leisure time, but because Gwen was so intrigued, I decided that I would humour her and we'd visit the inn for a cup of coffee.

The narrow road meandered for miles and miles. Higher and higher we climbed and eventually we reached Kirkstone Pass itself. It was a beautiful warm day, but I could imagine how barren and remote this place would feel in the depths of winter when the snow was falling. I had no doubt whatsoever that the residents of the area would at times be completely cut off from civilization, as the road would become impassable in bad weather.

We rounded a corner just before we reached the highest point and there at the side of the road ahead we could see a white building. There was a sign hanging outside and people were sitting at tables. We could see that there was a car park directly opposite on the other side of the narrow road. We drew into it and, leaving the car, crunched across the gravel towards the road. We crossed the road and entered the Kirkstone Pass Inn.

The atmosphere of the old inn was heavy laden with layer upon layer of events. Spirit activity was rife. Spirit people from different eras were coming and going. The amount of residual energy was overwhelming. I have visited many places, both large and small, grand and lowly, during my long career. The Kirkstone Pass Inn was right up there with the best of them.

I immediately picked up the emanations of an old woman – an old crone who had at one time lived in the area. She had undoubtedly used the inn as a stopping-off place on her weary travels. Legend has her noted as a witch who placed a curse on the building. I knew that this was untrue, that there was no basis to the story whatsoever. The people of her time had looked upon her with suspicion merely because she was old and decrepit and had been known to use the local herbs as efficacious medicines. No curse had been laid here either – that was merely a story handed down over the years and born out of superstition. Nevertheless I felt that at some time a priest had been brought to the inn in an effort to lift the supposed curse. His efforts had obviously been to no avail as no curse ever existed.

As I looked around I caught sight of the wraith of a large grey cat as it flitted across the room, only to disappear quickly through a doorway. It was a big cat and was probably very well known to the people who stopped off at the inn on a regular basis. Down the years I heard a woman's voice echo: 'Tarm! Tarm!' Was this the name of the cat or was she calling out to a long-gone man? Whoever she was referring to, 'Tom' or 'Tarm' had played a part in the rich fabric of the old inn's history.

Although it was a sunny Sunday afternoon, the ghosts of Kirkstone Pass Inn were very prevalent. I knew that phenomena would be experienced here on a regular basis. Clocks would no doubt stop or suddenly register the incorrect time, lights would flicker on and off and there was an area where it would always seem dark and oppressive – I suspected that this would be a bedroom. I gained the psychic impression that a girl's sobbing would sometimes be heard and then on other occasions childish laughter. This was all in the residual energy of the building. I also knew that people had at times felt a tugging at their clothes as they sat and imbibed the ales that the inn had to offer.

I stood in the room and opened myself up further to the spirit vibrations. I felt sure that the name 'Rose' or 'Rosemary' had played a part in the history of the building, although this spirit person was only one of the many souls return to the inn.

I gained the impression that at one time the inn had comprised two buildings, rather than the single building that it is today. I was sure that the years 1489, 1653, 1721–23 and 1869 had been notable years in its history and 19 July was significant in some way.

Now the names 'Emily' and 'Anna Perkins' echoed out. Different people from different times – a mish-mash of photographs in time.

My senses continued to be inundated with psychic impressions. The residual energies were so very strong here. A coffin had at some time been found hidden in a part of the building. Jealousy and intrigue had played its part in the past. I did not understand why, but I could see what looked like a group of smugglers huddled in a group making their secret plans. There had been a murder within the walls of the building too

– the inn was no stranger to tragic death. I felt the emanations of a tormented soul, grounded because of deeds committed and the fear of the spiritual payment to be made.

I moved towards the fireplace. As I did so, the shadow of a man, tall and dark, flitted from one corner to another. A landlord from times gone by maybe? I sensed witchcraft and occult practices, though I could detect nothing of an evil note.

I moved out of the inn and into the sunny late after-noon and walked to the end of the building. As I reached it and moved into the shadows, I became over-whelmed by a sense of deep sadness. I saw sheep, lambs and flowing water. Suddenly the water turned blood red – it was almost a river of blood. I felt a terrible sadness overcome me and felt the tremor of fear in my chest. Something sinister lingered here, although I knew not what. Still the water ran red, though there was no physical water near the area where I was stand-ing. The deep stream running in front of the inn was located on the other side of the road about 50 yards away.

Again I received impressions of witchcraft – this time of the black arts. I could not understand the impressions I was receiving in this idyllic and remote part of Cumbria.

Gwen and I decided that we would continue our journey home. This meant turning the car round and retracing our path down the narrow meandering road towards Windermere, some five or six miles distant.

After driving for around a mile I began to feel unwell. I felt almost faint and knew that I had to pull the car into a safe place as soon as I possibly could.

Gwen was concerned and wondered whether the heat of the day had caused me to feel so ill. I pointed out to her that the vehicle we were in was air conditioned and that we had not been sitting out in the sun for very long, much less time than I would normally stay in the sunshine. Gwen had eaten exactly the same food as I had, so we knew that it was not food poisoning. In spite of all the logical reasons Gwen came up with for my sudden sickness, there was no explanation. I also had the strongest of feelings that my condition was more to do with psychic energies that any physical cause. I had been under psychic attack before and I remembered the signs all too well. I knew there and then that something in the Kirkstone Pass Inn had attached itself to me and was causing my feelings of sickness and disorientation.

I managed to negotiate the steep narrow road down through Kirkstone Pass itself and Gwen and I were both relieved to see ahead of us a small area of land, once muddy but now dry and parched, where I could pull the car off the road. There was a brick wall to one side of the road but the side into which we pulled was wooded, the trees stretching back some distance from the road. I switched off the engine of the car.

After sitting still for a short while, I began to feel a little better. Gwen noticed a small pathway through the trees and suggested that a walk in the cool shade of the trees might help me. I agreed.

Taking a bottle of water each from the car, we strolled along the pathway through the trees. It was pleasant and cool and I felt almost back to myself again.

We had walked no more than 100 yards through the trees, however, when we noticed that the atmosphere had begun to change. A wind had struck up and the daylight seemed to be dimming.

'Looks as though it's going to start raining,' Gwen commented. 'We'd better head back to the car before we get soaked.'

We turned around to retrace our steps. Ahead of us I could make out the outline of the car parked at the side of the road. The sun was still beating down on it, causing the black paintwork to glint and shine. How odd! I looked upwards but couldn't see the sky through the canopy of the trees. Nevertheless, the area in which we were now standing still had all the signs of a gathering storm. The lower branches of the trees were beginning to whip around in the wind and it was growing gloomier by the minute.

I grabbed hold of Gwen's arm. 'Stand still!' I told her.

We both stood and listened. All we could hear was the sound of the wind blowing through the leaves.

We had stood there for no more than a couple of moments when out of the corner of my eye I saw a movement between the tree trunks a few feet away from us. It was almost as though a figure was darting from tree to tree but attempting to keep itself hidden from sight. I concentrated further. I knew that this was no physical being.

'Sam!' I called upon my spirit guide. 'What's going on here?'

Sam told me that the sinister feeling that I had experienced outside the inn was the result of the spirit of a woman known as Kate. She had not been present at the time of my visit, but I had picked up on her residual energy. In her physical life she had practised the black arts and had been feared by all who had come into contact with her. If anybody had a grievance against their neighbour and wanted to bring havoc into their lives, Kate was the person they would get in touch with.

Now this spirit woman had become aware of my visit to the Kirkstone Pass Inn and had hastened to meet me. She was afraid that I was visiting to attempt to rid the surrounding area of her presence and that is why she had attempted to disarm me by making me feel ill.

I stared through the trees once more, seeking out the shape I had noted a few moments earlier. Then from behind one of the tree trunks there stepped a woman of medium height and build. She wore a long dark shawl around her shoulders and the skirt of her dress almost reached the floor, but the hem was ragged and mud smeared. She wore a dark covering on her head of a fashion that I had never seen before. It could not be described as a bonnet or a mobcap. Wisps of grey hair had escaped from this head covering and, although the woman did not look old, I realized that she was not a young person. I would judge her to have been in her late forties. She certainly did not look sinister – she did not fulfil the generally accepted description of somebody who practised black magic, but I knew from her emanations that she was a powerful spirit. If left alone, she would harm no one but, if threatened, she could cause untold problems in a person's life.

I had no wish to tangle with her. I was aware of the fact that I was not feeling as strong as I normally would and, added to that, I had Gwen with me. We were some way away from our vehicle and in a remote part of the country with nobody around should we need help. Somehow I had to reason with Kate's spirit so that she would allow us to get back into our car and go on our way safely.

I knew that long experience of accompanying me on investigations had alerted Gwen to the fact that all was not well. I also knew that her own psychic senses had told her that there was something amiss.

'Is there somebody around here?' she asked.

I nodded. 'Yes there is, but I am not going to take this person on. I am not going to go into battle with this spirit because I don't feel strong enough, but we have to get away – now!'

'You don't have to say any more than that,' Gwen said as she began to hurry in the direction of the roadway and what she considered to be the safety of the car.

I knew that things were not quite as simple as that. Kate had the power to endanger our lives whilst driving home. She was powerful enough to cause a mechanical malfunction or even to affect my driving capability enough to cause an accident. She had to be placated.

By now Gwen had almost reached the side of the road. I turned to face the spirit of Kate. I spoke to her in reasonable tones and assured her that I had not entered what she considered to be her territory in order to cause her upset in any way. I told her that we were doing nothing more than having a pleasant drive out and had visited Kirkstone Pass Inn through nothing more than curiosity. I certainly had not come in order to disturb any spirit presence there and definitely not to attempt to move her on from the area around the inn which she considered to be her own personal domain.

Kate stood still. I knew that she was listening to my whispered words.

I continued, 'I recognize your power and am grateful that you have used only a tiny portion of that power against me. I ask that you allow me and my wife to leave here in peace.'

After a few moments of standing stock still, Kate slowly inclined her head in a nod of agreement. She had spoken not one word to me.

Gradually she began to fade. As she did so, I noted that the wind that had caused the branches of the trees to thrash around diminished to nothing more than a light summer breeze. Sunlight began to dapple the ground – it was as though a dark cloud had passed across the face of the sun and moved on.

I walked back down the pathway to join Gwen, who was standing next to the car.

'That was all very strange,' she commented.

I told her about Kate and the fact that for once in my life I had not engaged a spirit in battle.

'Hmmm! Just as well you didn't!' came the reply.

There are times in our lives when we have to let matters be. I do not condone any evil intent, whether it is from a person in physical or spirit form, and I will spend my lifetime working for the good and positive aspects of human life and afterlife. On this occasion, however, the only sensible thing to do was to walk away.

CHAPTER TEN

Human Tragedy

Liverpool city centre is home to many ghosts from the past. The city has been no stranger to tragedy over the years.

I am obviously no stranger to the city centre, having spent my youth visiting various clubs and nightspots and of course working there in later years when I had my office in Victoria Street. In spite of this I am ashamed to say that I know little of the history of my home town, having carefully avoided any efforts to educate me on this subject in favour of attending football practice for my school team!

I have often walked down Paradise Street, however, after parking my car in the multi-storey car park there and visiting the local radio station, Radio Merseyside, who had their studio there. Over the years I have seen old buildings disappear and new ones take their place – all in the name of progress. The memories of those buildings remain, however, in the residual energies of the ground upon which they once stood. Even though a building has long gone, if the events that took place there held a strong enough emotion, those memories will be as clear to a medium as if they happened yester-day and the building was still standing.

I am often asked to investigate locations in various towns and cities. Indeed, a television programme, *Derek Acorah's Ghost Towns*, has been developed for me by LIVINGtv, where I visit various buildings – shops, homes, theatres, etc. – in an effort to unravel the para-normal events that have been reported there. Liverpool is no different and I take the greatest of pleasure in helping to solve mysteries and rescue souls who may be grounded or lost in this big city.

I had been asked to guest on a Radio Merseyside programme, *The Billy Butler Show*. I had known Billy for many years, from the days when I used to guest on *The Billy & Wally Show* every Friday morning for another local radio station, Radio City. Billy had since moved on and now had a regular slot with Radio Merseyside.

After the show I left the building and was just about to cross the road to collect my car from the car park when I was stopped by a young man who introduced himself as Jed.

'I've been listening to you on Billy's show and thought I'd walk around to ask you whether you'd come and have a look at our shop,' he told me.

He explained that he worked in a shop just around the corner in Manesty's Lane – in fact it was on the corner of Paradise Street and Manesty's Lane. I was not in a rush, so I agreed to go along to see whether I could help him.

We walked the few yards to his place of work, which was a newish building with lots of large glass windows. Jed walked me through to the rear of the shop and as he did so he explained that although the shop staff had not reported anything untoward, the security staff who took over at night were telling a different story. Each night after the shop had closed and the doors been locked, the night staff heard moans and groans, shrieks and cries of anguish. Stock had been inexplicably moved and one security guard had fled, never to return, after saying that he had seen a number of spectral children lying there with their heads and limbs grotesquely twisted.

I could not begin to imagine what was the cause of all this. My memories of that part of the city in the years before refurbishment were vague. All I could recall was some old buildings that had been maybe warehouses or old offices. Prior to the car park being built, this was not a street that I had frequented, the area where the clubs were located being further down towards Seel Street and Bold Street.

I stood in the rear room of the shop and opened myself up to the psychic vibrations. I was more than surprised to pick up emanations of laughter and gaiety, dancing girls and bawdy songs of the Victorian era. I could hear the sound of many voices raised in song. In fact the picture unfolding before me reminded me very much of a programme I had seen many years ago entitled *The Good Old Days*, where a Victorian theatre scenario had been re-created for television. It was a fascinating spectacle.

Slowly the picture faded, to be replaced by pandemonium. People were running and screaming. I heard the cry of 'Fire!' ring out. I felt knocked and buffeted, as though I was standing in the path of a large crowd of people – men, women and children – as they fled from an unseen danger. I felt myself staggering. Vaguely I heard Jed's voice asking anxiously, 'Are you alright, Derek?' but I couldn't answer. I was gasping for breath. The pressure of the residual energy of the panicking crowd was so great that it forced me to stagger backwards until my back was pressed against the wall. The pressure on my chest was so great that even though I opened my mouth wide in an attempt to draw breath, no air could get into my lungs. I tried to raise my arms to clutch at my throat, but I couldn't do it. It was as though they were pinned to my side by the pressure of the energy. Then, complete blackness!

I awoke lying on the floor with Jed leaning over me, shaking my shoulder. 'Derek! Derek! Are you OK?' he was asking frantically.

'I'm alright … I think,' I told him shakily. 'I don't know what happened on this ground, but it still retains the memory and energy of a great tragedy.'

I clambered to my feet and leaned against the wall. It was obvious that whatever had gone on had had terrible consequences, because the residual energy was still so strong within the building. Even though the construction was relatively new, the ground upon which it was built still held the memories of what had taken place. It had to have been a major tragedy for the emanations to be so strong and for me to have been affected so badly.

I was able to tell Jed that what the night staff had experienced was not the work of a malicious spirit, nor was it due to any spirit attempting to draw attention to itself. It was merely the replaying of a memory – a photograph in time – captured forever in that spot. I was unsure exactly what had happened, but I suggested that he might like to attempt a little research based on the facts that I had given him.

Some weeks later Jed e-mailed me to tell me that he had done as I had suggested and had discovered that the spot upon which the shop now stood had once been the Colosseum Theatre, which had been well known as a music hall. One night in October 1878 the theatre had been packed out with some 4,000 people. During the performance a cry of 'Fire!' had gone up. This had caused the audience to rise *en masse* and head for the doors in order to escape. Men, women and children had been crushed to death in their desperate effort to get to the doorway and out onto the street. In all, 37 people had left their physical lives that night due to being trampled and crushed. The greatest tragedy of all was that it had all been the result of a false alarm!

Never before had I been affected so deeply by residual energy alone. Normally I would have expected a spirit presence to engender the effect that I experienced that day, but never a memory in time. That was before I visited Pearl Harbor.

I had always wanted to visit Pearl Harbor in Honolulu on the Hawaiian Islands and was fortunate enough to be able to do this during a holiday break quite recently. Pearl Harbor is, of course, the place where so many US servicemen lost their lives when bombed by Japan at 7.55 a.m. on Sunday 7 December 1941, thus commencing America's involvement in World War II. USS *Oklahoma*, *West Virginia*, *Helena*, *Utah*, *Tennessee*, *California* and *Arizona* were either bombed or torpedoed during those fateful hours, resulting in the loss of over 1,700 lives.

The taxi ride to the museum and memorial through the hot sun of Honolulu was pleasant, but as Gwen and I got out I was immediately affected by a tremendous pressure in my head. My temples throbbed in pain. I had not expected this. I hadn't thought for a moment that I would be effectively 'opened up' involuntarily by the wealth of emotion contained in the area. This was due, of course, not only to the events that had taken place on that fateful day but also to the emotions of the millions of people who had visited the memorial since it had been opened in 1963.

I do not know quite what I expected when I visited the USS *Arizona* memorial. Gwen and I walked through the car park to a tent where hand baggage had to be deposited – part of the heavy security surrounding the area. We then walked along to the museum area, where a video of the terrible events was running. There were photographs and artefacts and a model of the ill-fated *Arizona* which had sunk, taking so many young lives with it into the sunlit harbour. There was also the spent carcass of a Japanese torpedo and glass cases containing the pathetic few personal effects that had once belonged to some of those whose bodies still lie beneath the peaceful waters.

We walked down to the water's edge to an area that had once lain beneath water level but had since been land-filled to create a memorial garden. There were plinths with boards telling the story of Pearl Harbor and listing the names of the men who had lost their lives on that day.

The time came for us to board a small launch that would take us across the bay to the memorial building itself, which spanned the rusting remains of the *Arizona* at permanent rest just beneath the water's surface, its turrets still visible above the water, a tribute to the 1,102 shipmates entombed there. The structure was a curious affair that sagged in the centre but stood strong at the ends, evidently to express initial defeat and then ultimate victory.

We were both struck by the solemn calm and depth of feeling in that marble-floored creation. The only sound to be heard was the click of heels as people walked from marble tablet to marble tablet, each inscribed with the names of the people who had perished. Tears sprung to my eyes. I felt deep sadness and an enormous sense of loss – the loss of the hopes and dreams of all the 1,177 crewmen who died aboard the *Arizona* and their families, who had come to visit their memorial. The sound of feet as they moved slowly across the floor deepened the sense of sombre but reverent calm. Silently people absorbed the church-like atmosphere before making their way back to the launch, each one lost in their own private world of remembrance and new-found reverence for those who had been lost.

We boarded the launch once more and travelled the short distance back across the water to the mainland. As I stepped onto the jetty I was suddenly overcome by a feeling of intense pain down the side of my face. I almost cried out loud. My hand shot to my face and I had the impression of a gaping wound and blood rushing through my fingers.

'Are you OK?' Gwen asked, peering up at me worriedly.

'I don't know,' I answered weakly. 'I feel as though I have been shot in the face and neck.'

Gwen led me to a bench where we sat down so that I could collect myself. I attempted to gather my thoughts. What I was doing was picking up on the residual energy of the terrible massacre that had taken place in 1941. As I struggled to regain control of the situation, I received impressions of wave after wave of Japanese bombers streaming through the morning sky to fling their missiles on the American fleet. As though from a great distance, I could hear massive explosions. I could sense pandemonium and terror. The time of the attack was measured in moments in my life, but it endured for two hours in reality – two hours that would change the world.

I closed myself down to the emanations and atmosphere of the area, feeling thoroughly drained by what I had experienced.

Gwen and I walked back towards the museum and gift-shop area. Sitting at a desk signing books was an old man. He was slim and wiry in build. On his head he wore a peaked cap bearing the legend 'Arizona Survivor'. I walked towards him and shook his hand. His bright blue eyes twinkled. I wondered what sights he had witnessed and how he managed to look so cheerful. 'Howdy, son!' he greeted me.

As I clasped his hand, I had no words but what I did see standing beside him was a spirit man, cheerful and happy, who saluted me smartly and grinned. I don't suppose the old man will ever know in this lifetime that his chum Edwin, lost to the waters of Pearl Harbor, spends time with him, but no doubt in the years to come they will be reunited.

Chapter Eleven

Possessed

'Possession' is a word that is often used by people who are ignorant about the channelling of a spirit by a medium. I have lost count of the number of times that I have been asked about 'when I was possessed'. Once again, I reiterate that I have never been 'possessed'. I have channelled deeply and have allowed a spirit person to overshadow me so that I may portray the exact personality of that entity, but I have never, ever been possessed in the true sense of the word.

The true state of possession is when a person, either purposely or inadvertently, allows a spirit entity to take complete charge of their body and mind. The literature on this subject is legion and dates back into the mists of time. Have you ever wondered why you were told as a child to cover your mouth when you yawned? Originally, it was not due to social politeness, but the fact that it was believed that whilst your mouth was wide open a spirit could jump in and take over your entire being – hence you would be possessed. I often smile to myself when I imagine an ether full of nasty spirits just waiting for a person to yawn in order to leap into their body and take it over. That, of course, is nonsense. It is the person's *mind* that has to be open – an individual has to be in a certain state of mind before a spirit entity can have the opportunity to take over their personality.

It is interesting to note that when a person is possessed, there is more likelihood of physical alteration to the features. This, of course, is not to be confused with trance mediumship, where again a medium is merely channelling a spirit and is in a state of deep meditation.

It is also interesting to note that when a person is taken over by a spirit, that entity is more likely to be of the lower realms than of the higher, more angelic ones. I believe that this is because spirits dwelling closer to our physical world are less evolved – they are people who were responsible for atrocities against humanity when in their physical life.

It is unfortunate that in some cases where a person has suffered a sickness of the mind they are left vulnerable to attack and possession by these evil spirit entities. I came across one such case many years ago. It was an experience I will never forget. It was the first time that I had ever come face to face with a truly evil spirit invading the personality and body of a vulnerable human being.

A woman called me at my office in Liverpool. She told me and that her name was Mrs Taylor and I had been recommended to her by somebody who had suggested that I might be able to help with her problem. She went to great lengths to explain to me that normally she would not bother with spiritualists and mediums, but she was at the end of her tether because of her daughter Lynne.

Mrs Taylor explained that Lynne had been a normal, happy child who had done very well at school and had gone on to university, where she had been studying law. She had decided that rather than move into student accommodation she would remain living with her parents, as their home was only a matter of a few miles from the university. Everything had been going well and she had been enjoying her life as a student.

'I don't know what happened, but Lynne suddenly changed,' Mrs Taylor went on. 'From being a bright, outgoing girl who took part in all the social life of the uni, she suddenly became quiet and introverted. She started doing some very out of character things – in fact it seemed as though she wasn't our Lynne anymore.' Mrs Taylor's voice sank to a whisper and I could hear that she was crying – it was almost as though she was afraid to go on. 'Will you help us, Derek?' she pleaded desperately. 'My husband and I just don't know what to do.'

It was November, it was wet and cold and rapidly growing darker. I thought longingly of my warm home and the football match I was looking forward to watching. The desperation in the woman's voice, however, was such that I could not ignore it. 'I'll pop over to see you,' I told her. 'I'll be there in an hour or so.'

It was dark when I eventually reached the address given to me by Mrs Taylor. It was a neat suburb in the older part of town where all of the houses were Victorian. Mrs Taylor's family home was quite large but had a neglected air about it. It was almost as though the owners had left. The garden was now a little overgrown and sad.

As I walked up the path and approached the front door, I was surprised to see that the windows were all smashed and had been boarded up from the inside. The front door was the same – the glass panel had been smashed and a piece of wood covered the gap. I was beginning to think that I had been sent on a wild goose chase, but then I noticed a glimmer of light through the slats of wood.

I knocked on the door. After a few moments it was opened and I introduced myself.

'Oh, thank goodness you've come, Derek. I can't thank you enough. I'm really so sorry about the state of the place, but ...' Mrs Taylor dissolved once more into tears.

As I entered the house I could not help but notice that it looked as though vandals had been in and wrecked the place. There was also a very unclean smell permeating the air, which somebody had unsuccessfully tried to mask with floral air-freshener.

Mrs Taylor led me along the hallway and into a room where a gentleman was sitting. 'This is Bill, my husband,' she said.

The room, although large, contained no more than a couple of plain easy chairs and a sofa with a small coffee table in front of it. I was invited to take a seat, which I did. Mr and Mrs Taylor then proceeded to tell me exactly what had been going on.

They explained that it was as though they had lost their daughter. Although there was still a vague physical resemblance to the lovely young girl they had known, the person who now shared their house with them was nothing short of evil. Mr Taylor said that Lynne's out of character behaviour had started happening whilst she was studying hard for her examinations. Things got progressively worse, to the point where Mr and Mrs Taylor knew that they had no alternative but to seek medical help. They were almost certain that there was nothing physically wrong with Lynne, so were not surprised when she was immediately referred for psychiatric assessment. In spite of heavy medication, her condition had continued to deteriorate and the doctor had suggested that the best solution would be for her to be certified and placed in a mental health unit.

'We couldn't do that, though, Derek!' Mrs Taylor told me. 'Not to our Lynne. Just occasionally we see glimpses of the girl she used to be and we know that somehow, in some way, we will get our daughter back.'

I asked whether I could meet Lynne and was told that just prior to my arrival she had fallen asleep. Her mother was reluctant to wake her, as the times when she was actually asleep were the only small oases of peace and calm that she and her husband could grasp. At all other times one of them had to be awake and looking out for their daughter.

'You must be wondering about the state of the house,' Bill remarked. 'Believe me, it wasn't always like this. We used to have a normal, comfortable home, but Lynne has ruined everything. When she gets into one of her worst states it's nothing for her to smash windows, doors and furniture. It's pointless replacing the broken glass in the windows, because we know it will only be smashed once more within a day or two. All the doors have to be securely bolted, otherwise she will just go out. The windows have to be securely covered too, because she would be perfectly happy to just climb out of one of them, regardless of the sharp glass which would cut her to ribbons.'

Mr Taylor took me upstairs to show me Lynne's bedroom. If the conditions were bad downstairs, they were even worse up here.

There was no bed – that had long since been smashed to pieces. 'She got that she wouldn't sleep in it anyway,' said her father. 'She just curls up on a duvet, just like a dog. That's when she actually goes to sleep,' he added wryly.

There was a large wardrobe, marked and damaged by what looked like nails scoring over the once polished surface, and a battered-looking chair. Just as downstairs, the windows of the room were covered in sheets of wood nailed securely to prevent them from being pulled off. The worst thing about the room, though, was the fact that the walls were smeared with faeces. Yet there had been an obvious attempt to keep everything clean because the floral wallpaper had almost been scrubbed away in places.

We returned to the sitting room to speak further. I felt desperately sorry for the two people sitting in front of me. They were loving parents who wanted nothing more than normality with their only daughter. They loved her to pieces and were not willing to see her incarcerated for what could well turn out to be a very long time.

I quailed at the task before me. I knew that this was something that I could not deal with on my own. 'I will do my best to help you,' I told Lynne's parents, 'but this is a situation where I will require the assistance of another person. I have a great friend, Ken Swindells, who is an extremely strong and experienced medium. He is also a healer. It is my opinion that the combination of his guides, guardians and inspirers and mine will see an end to the purgatory you are all suffering.'

Mr and Mrs Taylor agreed to allow me to bring Ken along with me the following day when our work would begin and I left them to endure another night of caring for Lynne.

On my way home I called in to see Ken to ask him whether he would be kind enough to accompany me the following day. Just as expected, he had no reservations whatsoever.

'And what did you pick up from the atmosphere whilst you were in the house, Derek?' he asked.

I told him that I had never ever experienced the degree of hatred, evil and horror that emanated from the fabric of the home. I told him that I knew there was something demonic residing there on an almost permanent basis. This demonic being was in almost total control of the poor young girl. He had homed in on her sensitivity at a time when she was both mentally and physically depleted whilst studying for her examinations. Now he would not easily be repelled and she was far too weak to do anything about it. He had drained her of all her energy and was using her as a puppet. He would not easily let go.

All the time I was speaking, Ken sat with his eyes closed, absorbing my words. When I had finished, he sat bolt upright. 'We must help the young lady,' he stated firmly. 'Whoever – or whatever – will not win!'

I thanked Ken. I was very grateful for his help. I knew that if there was anybody I could rely upon at a time like this it was him. He had 50 years' experience of working with spirit under his belt. I could ask for no better.

The following day I drove to Ken's home to collect him and then we both travelled to the home of Mr and Mrs Taylor to come face to face with this visitor from the lower regions who had taken over their daughter.

Mr Taylor opened the door to our first knock. He led us down the hallway and through to the room in which I had been sitting the previous evening. Sitting on the sofa was Lynne. I knew who she was because her father introduced us as we entered the room, but otherwise I would not have known the person before me was a young woman. She was pale with a greyish blotchy look about her skin, the clothes she wore hung on her frame and her long dark hair hung down her back and around her face in the manner of a crone – greasy, dull and straggly. The cuffs of her cardigan fell down almost to her knuckles and her hands were red and sore looking, with grubby broken nails. I could see that she was rail thin – she had no physical substance at all.

As we walked further into the room, Lynne suddenly seemed to notice us. Slowly she raised her head and looked directly at me. Her eyes, which had moments before looked lacklustre and vacant, suddenly blazed with an inhuman light. She said nothing.

I felt Ken move close up behind me. 'Ask for a name,' he said.

The hairs on the back of my neck stood on end as Lynne, head thrown back, mouth wide open, showing blackened teeth, broke into unearthly and demonic laughter.

Just as suddenly as the laughter started, it stopped. I now had the full attention of the being who was invading Lynne's body. Those strange eyes were riveted on my face.

'Who are you?' I asked. 'Why are you here?'

Through tight lips and in a cracked though strong voice the being replied, 'Don't you know, Derek Acorah?'

There followed more laughter, which just as abruptly came to a halt.

After a few moment's silence the same gravelly voice said, 'I'd like to dance. Dance with me, Derek Acorah!'

Lynne stood up and began walking towards me.

I could hear Sam talking to me. 'Don't back down, Derek. This is no time to show fear. You have to be strong. I am here with your gatekeepers. Ken is here with the strength of his guides and inspirers. Have faith. You will come to no harm.'

Lynne had reached a point directly in front of me. I had a great deal of difficulty in preventing myself from retching at the odour emanating from her body. We took each other's arms and began a slow sedate waltz around the sitting room. I knew that I was not dancing with Lynne, but was progressing around the room in the arms of the being who was controlling her. Although the young woman's body was almost skin and bone, I could feel the steely strength and vitality of this being's physical power. I was afraid. I knew that

161

this demonic spirit had insisted that I dance to let me know that we were not dealing with some weak, easily banished entity.

I looked towards Ken as Lynne and I continued to waltz slowly around. He was standing with his eyes closed. I knew that he was summoning up the strength of his spiritual helpers.

Suddenly his eyes opened. 'Do you want to stop dancing now?' he asked in a pleasant and calm voice.

As he spoke, he walked towards Lynne and me and took hold of one of her arms, leaving me holding the other. The strength I had felt earlier seemed to double and we were almost thrown to the floor as we tried to stand in the middle of the room. Ken started to call out to our guides and helpers to assist us in ejecting this evil entity from the body of Lynne. I joined in with him whilst we both held on tightly to her arms. We also called upon Lynne's own spiritual doorkeepers to help us rid her of the evil being who was presently control-ling her.

After some minutes, the struggling became less and we were able to guide Lynne over to the sofa, where she suddenly flopped down and fell asleep. We continued our prayers, calling out to the powers beyond to help in permanently ridding Lynne of the wicked entity who had taken her over.

Without warning the room suddenly seemed to go cold. 'Don't stop, Derek,' Ken demanded. 'Keep on going.'

We sat for a few moments longer, sending out our thoughts and prayers for Lynne to be released. I knew because of the drop in temperature that we were surrounded by helpers from the spirit world who had congregated to help remove this invading evil presence from Lynne's life forever.

Suddenly Lynne seemed to slump even further down on the sofa. I looked more closely at her and realized that she was indeed asleep, but now she had a relaxed look about her and there was a certain pinkness to her skin that definitely hadn't been present before. She was breathing evenly and looked utterly relaxed.

Ken called to Mr and Mrs Taylor, who had been sitting in the kitchen, to come through. When they saw Lynne asleep on the sofa Mrs Taylor gasped in amazement. 'Look at her!' she exclaimed. 'She actually looks peaceful. Normally when she's asleep she's tossing and turning, twitching and moving all the time. I can't believe my eyes!'

Ken and I returned to the home of Mr and Mrs Taylor for four more days to cleanse the house of any residual energy of the demonic entity who had been making their lives miserable and also to conduct spiritual healing upon Lynne. It was only after that length of time that we both felt happy that we had returned the evil one to his rightful place on the astral plane – that place designated for spirits who have committed horrendous crimes against humanity.

After that, Mr and Mrs Taylor kept in touch with me for a long time. They were delighted at the progress back to good health that Lynne began making from that day onwards.

Now Lynne is fully recovered and has been for many years. Alas, Ken Swindells has since passed on to the spirit world. He was one of the most miraculous healers I have ever had the pleasure of working with, but the day came when his work was done and it was time for him to leave. I have no doubt whatsoever that Ken will be continuing with his healing from the other side of life.

So you can see that when people speak about me being 'possessed', they really do not know what they are talking about. If they had ever been in the company of somebody whose life had been taken over by the spirit of another, they would instantly recognize that what I do is no more than channelling a spirit entity.

CHAPTER TWELVE

Nearly the Death of Me

My British theatre tour was coming to an end and my thoughts were turning towards my holiday break. I was looking forward to a very relaxing cruise to the Caribbean Islands. Gwen was looking forward to the holiday too, because she had been working very hard throughout the year.

We flew into Miami in the early afternoon, then transferred to our hotel for the night, feeling more than a little jet lagged. We retired to bed early and the following morning were collected and taken to our cruise ship. We were shown to our cabin, where we settled in. Then, after showering and changing, we went to one of the restaurants on board for dinner.

The following morning we walked around the ship in order to acquaint ourselves fully with the layout. Although the weather was warm, the ocean was surprisingly choppy. The movement of the ship had caused many of our fellow travellers to remain in their cabins. Both Gwen and I hoped that things would improve as we headed further south.

The next day proved to be a little sunnier. I walked up to the sun deck, lay down on one of the loungers and soon dropped off into a light snooze. I can't have been dozing for more than a few minutes when I was woken by the sound of a man talking. I realized that although I couldn't see anybody, he was actually talking to me, and in rather a rude manner.

'Oh dear!' I thought to myself. Here was I on holiday, trying to relax, but still having spirit people communicating with me – and without prompting. Gwen, who was sitting at a table close by, noticed my expression and asked me what was wrong. I told her that I had just heard a man's voice speaking to me and that he was rather a foul-mouthed individual too. I knew that Gwen would be remembering only too well an occasion on another trip when a spirit man had forced me to seek out his relatives in order to tell them that he was happy and well. I also knew that she would be less than pleased if those circumstances were to be repeated. So I spoke in my mind to the man, asking him to leave me alone. He replied quite clearly, telling me that he would be back later whether I liked it or not. I quietly asked Sam to intervene.

A few more days passed and I forgot all about the rather rude spirit man who had interrupted my snooze in the sun. We had reached an island that was only accessible by ship's tender. It was on board the tender that I heard the spirit man's voice again. This time he was less rude, but he was trying to persuade me not to make the trip to shore.

'If you go, you'll have a bad accident,' he told me. 'You'll end up in a wheelchair for the rest of your holiday!'

Again I communicated with him mentally, asking him to leave me alone and telling him that my spirit guide Sam would take care of me and would warn me of any dangers ahead.

I was more than a little irritated. I close myself down purposely to interruptions when not working and especially when I am on holiday. Also, I was not at all happy with the personality of the man who was communicating with me. I felt that he could well be saying things that were incorrect and designed to cause me anxiety.

We finally reached the quay and disembarked from the small tender. We took a trip to see the popular tourist sights of the island before returning to one of the harbour cafés for lunch. Afterwards we took a stroll along the dusty seafront road.

After a while we stopped for a cold drink. As I was sitting there I spotted what seemed to be an old wooden building. I suggested that we walk up and take a look at it.

We strolled up to it. The door was open, so I walked in. I could immediately sense two spirit energies moving around the building. They did not seem at all concerned by my presence as they ambled around. I sensed that they were both male and seemed to have some sort of physical disability. I felt that they had both at some time in their physical lives been seamen.

There was nothing to be seen in the building – it was nothing more than a dilapidated and desolate wooden house that at some time had no doubt been home to somebody. I turned to leave, but as I did so I somehow lost my footing and fell forward and down through the front doorway.

Gwen, who had remained waiting outside, helped me up. 'What happened there?' she asked me.

'I don't know. It was not a normal trip – I felt as though I'd been pushed,' I replied.

I was unharmed apart from a small bruise on my arm, but just as we began walking back down the seafront road I heard a voice telling me, 'Next time I will do it properly!' I recognized the voice of the spirit man from the ship.

I told Gwen what I had heard. She looked at me askance. 'Are you sure? Tell him to go away! And ask Sam to have a word, because this could get dangerous. I think we'd better go back to the ship.'

I agreed.

The tender was on one of its final runs back to the ship, which was anchored a mile or so offshore. It drew up alongside the ship and people started climbing out and onto the gangway leading back on board. The sea was quite choppy, which meant that the tender was bobbing up and down and everybody had to choose their moment to step back onto the gangway. Two members of crew were assigned to help each person alight.

As my turn came to be helped up the steps of the tender, I put my arm out to one of the crew members for him to help me. Suddenly, an elderly man who had been impatiently waiting behind me lurched forward to try to jump the queue and get ahead of me. At that moment the tender went down on a wave and the man's right leg was on the gangway and his left leg still on the final step of the tender. He lost his balance and if it had not been for the two crewmen, who quickly pulled him away from the tender, he would have been jammed between the side of the ship and the side of the tender and badly injured.

I wondered privately whether this near-accident had been meant for me. Had it not been for the impatient man pushing his way forward suddenly, I would have been the one who could have been badly hurt. I decided there and then that I would be very careful over the coming days.

At our evening meal that night, Gwen and I discussed with our table companions what we had done that day. As we were doing so, the soup course arrived. As I placed my spoon into the soup dish, the dish suddenly moved dramatically to the left.

'What happened then, Derek?' said the man sitting opposite me.

I laughed the incident off, saying that I must have caught the tablecloth accidentally. However, I knew that the spirit man was up to his tricks again.

After our dinner we strolled along to one of the entertainment lounges. We remained there for the next couple of hours, listening to music and generally enjoying the relaxed atmosphere. Just before midnight we decided to return to our cabin. After retiring for the night, I decided that it was time for a conversation with Sam.

Sam told me that he had been keeping track of the annoying spirit man who had apparently been following Gwen and me everywhere that we went. I asked him to talk to this soul and to establish why he was doing what he was doing.

Eventually I drifted off to sleep. I don't know how long I had been asleep when I was woken by a noise. I opened my eyes. In the dim light of the room I could make out a black shadowy figure hovering on the ceiling directly above me.

As I stared upwards, the black mass began to move around erratically. Suddenly all the breath was knocked out of my body. It was as though something heavy had dropped suddenly onto my chest. I could not speak. I frantically shouted out in my mind for Sam, calling out his name over and over again. I was very close to collapse.

Once more Sam's presence came around me. I could sense frenzied spirit activity – almost as though Sam was grappling with the dark entity. I heard his voice loudly and forcefully demanding, 'Go back now! Leave this place!' Then the room became peaceful and calm once more as the dark energies dispersed.

Gwen had been woken by my sudden movement on the bed and she switched on the overhead lights. I told her what had happened. 'This is too much!' she said.

I sat up in bed and as I did so Gwen asked what the red marks were on my chest. I looked down and sure enough, the whole of my upper chest area was covered in a large red mark.

With our sleep well and truly broken, we both sat discussing what had happened.

'Can't Sam do anything to get rid of the entity?' Gwen asked me. 'Can't he tell you why all this is going on and why he seems to want to harm you?'

Dawn was beginning to streak the skies before we finally fell asleep once more. Fortunately there were no further disturbances.

* * *

The following day was to be spent at sea. Gwen and I made full use of the wonderful spa facilities offered by the ship. By mid-afternoon I was ambling along to the sun-deck coffee shop, where I was to meet up with Gwen when she returned from the hair salon. I knew that I had around 30 minutes to kill. I sat down and enjoyed looking out at the horizon. It was totally relaxing sitting there in the warm sun.

At about the time when Gwen was due to join me I ordered coffee for us both. Fifteen minutes later she still had not arrived, so I decided that I would stroll up to the deck where the hair salon was. I chose to take an outdoor route along the deck and up the exterior staircase rather than take the stairs or lift inside the body of the ship. I walked along, eventually arriving at a point where the walkway was covered but there were large square openings along the length of the covered section. I stopped and leaned against the rail looking out to sea.

As I stood there, I once more heard the voice of the spirit man calling my name. It seemed to be coming from one of the openings a little further along the deck. I walked in that direction and on reaching the area leaned once more on the railing, looking to see where the voice had come from. There was nothing. All I could hear was the slap of the waves against the bulk of the ship's sides.

As I released my grip on the railing and was about to continue walking along the deck, I felt a huge push in the middle of my back, launching me in the direction of one of the large openings. The force was such that before I managed to stop myself, the top half of my body was hanging out of the opening. It was only the fact that I managed to grab hold of the railing again that prevented me from falling completely over the side and into the ocean.

I gathered my wits and made hastily towards a doorway leading to the interior of the ship. 'What next?' I thought to myself. I was now seriously concerned. I had come very close to being forced overboard and being lost at sea.

When I met up with Gwen she could see that I was disturbed and asked me what had happened. When I told her, she was appalled. 'What can you do, Derek?' she asked. 'This is getting a bit too dangerous.'

After coffee we returned once more to our cabin. We both wanted to watch an information video that the ship was running giving details of the following day's island visit.

As we sat watching the video, me on a chair and Gwen on the bed, an enormous crashing sound came from the bathroom. We looked at one another. I ran to the bathroom, only to find all the bottles and jars from the shelves had been swept into the washbasin. I could distinctly sense the presence of spirit, but this was not a kindly spirit – it was the spirit of the man who had been so rude and who I was convinced had attempted to endanger my life earlier on deck.

Twice I shouted out into the atmosphere, 'Why are you doing this?'

After a few moments the spirit form of a man began to manifest. He was a man in his sixties, of quite an athletic physique. He had receding grey hair, but it was his eyes that transfixed me. They held the most violent expression that I had ever seen. He looked almost evil.

Once more I asked him to identify himself and I asked him why he was attaching himself to me.

'Now I'll speak, Mr Do Gooder spiritual man who helps people! Ha!' He laughed in a very nasty manner.

I shuddered at the sound.

178

The man in spirit went on. 'You came to our place where we were happy, me and my friend. You disturbed us. You succeeded in banishing my friend to the horrible lower regions. You got rid of him, but not me. Ever since I been watching and waiting for my opportunity. I have followed you many times. I blame you for separating me from my friend. I'm very unhappy because of you. You have to pay for this.'

He mentioned an investigation I had conducted at an old public house in Liverpool. I remembered it very well indeed. It had taken place some six months previously and had been a particularly gruelling investigation that had left me drained both mentally and physically, such was the strength of the two spirit men who had insisted on remaining grounded in the old pub. One was the particularly nasty spirit of William Miles. After an enormous effort on my part, he had been sent to the higher side of life for higher beings to deal with. Although I had known that he had another male spirit with him, I had not realized that this second spirit was so dangerous and evil.

'Remember Charles Seymour!' the voice rang out.

I now knew the whole story and the reason why this man was trying to cause me harm. I also knew that he was not nearly as strong a spirit presence as his friend William had been. Without William to support him, and with Sam's help, I would have no difficulty whatsoever in banishing Charles Seymour to the same place as his cohort.

I called Sam's name. The bathroom door swung open and I heard a loud banging noise on the wardrobe door. Startled, Gwen looked up from the video. I knew that Sam was with me. His infinite light moved towards the spirit presence of Charles Seymour. The light enveloped him and totally swallowed him. As I sent out my thoughts and offered my physical strength to Sam, it diminished and then was no more. Sam had done it again. He had taken the soul of Seymour to his rightful place in the world of spirit, there to atone for the horrible deeds he had committed whilst in his physical life.

I turned to Gwen. 'It's done!' I told her. 'We won't have any more problems.'

I felt happier than I had done all holiday. From the moment I had heard the voice of Charles Seymour to the time I had almost ended up in the ocean, I had known at the back of my mind that if I wasn't careful, that spirit man would be the death of me!

CHAPTER THIRTEEN

Satanic Sorcery

From time immemorial there has been a belief in the supernatural powers of witches and their craft. There is a popular and very wrong conception that all witches contract with negative energies to produce mayhem in the lives of those who cross them. When a picture of a witch is conjured up they are portrayed usually as women, and mostly old women at that, bent of back and ragged in appearance, with hairy warts, hooked noses and cackling laughter – that laughter being never more prevalent than when misfortune visits an enemy. Furthermore, they are said to transport themselves at night on broomsticks and 'bear the devil's mark'.

In the seventeenth century Matthew Hopkins, famously remembered as the Witchfinder General, made himself a very well-known and rich man by travelling the country torturing people who had been reported to him as dabbling in witchcraft. The most vulnerable people were usually old women living alone with only a cat or dog for company. It is interesting to note that in those times it was unusual for people to take on animals as pets, but for an old lady living alone sometimes her only comfort would be the company of a beloved cat or dog. Elderly village women were also likely to be well versed in the medicinal values of herbs and plants. They would often be approached by fellow villagers for a 'potion' to cure ills. It would only take one of these women to upset a neighbour to find the Witchfinder General knocking on her door and to be accused of witchcraft then dragged away to be tortured into confession.

Over recent years the perception of witches and their craft has altered dramatically. The witches of today, in the majority, claim to be 'white' or 'good' witches who practise their 'magic' for the common good. Their beliefs are not Christian based but rather embody pagan traditions.

Over the years that I have been a practising medium I have come into the company of witches and pagans on numerous occasions. I can therefore attest to the fact that to a man (or woman) these people have been some of the nicest, gentlest and most caring individuals you would wish to meet. They practise their belief system quietly and without fuss. They generally wish nothing more than to live their lives caring for and worshipping the environment in which they live. If there were more witches in the world it would surely be a better place.

It is interesting to note, though, that throughout history, books make little mention of 'white' witchcraft, with more emphasis being placed on witches of the negative variety who cast spells to cause illness and misfortune. Obviously not all witches in history had evil intent and, as I explained earlier, not all people accused of practising witchcraft were in fact doing any such thing. There were, however, occasions when the accusations were justly made!

Many years ago I can recall talking to a man who had spent a number of months serving out the last part of a prison sentence at HM Prison Lancaster. For those who may not be aware, part of Lancaster castle is given over to law courts and a working prison. This man, who for obvious reasons will remain anonymous, told me that there were many stories of strange and supernatural goings-on within the prison section of the castle. Inexplicable noises were regularly heard and there were one or two cells that prisoners absolutely refused to spend time in. It is my understanding of the prison system that whims are not be easily catered to, so there must have been some solid basis to it all for the prison authorities to actually take note of what the men under their jurisdiction had to say about the cells.

The man told me that anybody placed in the cells concerned heard strange moaning and groaning noises and experienced a feeling of absolute dread and despair. Considering that it was a prison full of men who were hardened to the vagaries of life and not easily scared by 'things that go bump in the night', I too was of the opinion that there was something paranormal going on in there.

The very fact that Lancaster castle is so old would indicate that there would be much residual energy therein. Not only that, but the castle featured as the place where 19 people were incarcerated in dungeons 30 feet below ground level whilst they awaited trial on accusations of witchcraft during the early seventeenth century. Ten of those people were hanged before a baying crowd on 20 August 1612. Amongst those who were held there were those who became famously known as the Pendle witches, two of whom were Old Mother Demdike and Old Chattox. These people were kept at the castle in a small dungeon for five months on a diet of bread and gruel.

My conversation with the ex-prisoner took place many years before I was first introduced to the Pendle witches during a live three-day television ghost-hunting extravaganza during my days as medium on LIVINGtv's programme *Most Haunted*. Such were my experiences over that three-day period that I was determined to return and I did, as part of the *Most Haunted* programme series, but the circumstances of that second visit were such that I could not open myself up properly to the emanations prevailing at the time. It has to be remembered that when a medium is working and 'open' to the atmosphere and emotions of a location, they not only pick up the residual energies and spiritual activity around them but also the feelings of the people who are physically present on the day, including those people's feelings towards them, and this will affect radically the level and quality of work that they produce. The moods and emotions of a television crew working around a medium will therefore affect the level of work produced by that medium. If the crew are fearful or nervous of what might happen during an investigation (because do not forget that they all know the history of the location whereas the medium does not), they may be prey to suggestion and will therefore expect to experience paranormal events. And if a crew member has less than kind thoughts and feelings towards the medium, this will manifest in an anger that the medium will pick up and be affected by.

I would like one day to go back to experience Pendle without television cameras, without the influence of other people and without the possibility of human interference, whether purposely or accidentally created.

In retrospect, I believe that the witches of Pendle were nothing more than a group of people who in today's terms would be labelled 'neighbours from hell'. They were poor, of low intellect and possibly a little dishonest, and the older members of the family probably practised the age-old art of herbalism. They were certainly vicious in temperament – that I do know from my 'meeting' with them during the programme – but who can wonder at it? Their experiences at the hands of people acting on behalf of the law of the country would hardly leave their spirits with pleasant memories of their time here on Earth. The spirit souls of these people no doubt wish to wreak vengeance upon anybody who attempts to invoke them at the sites of their physical lifetimes. When I visit Pendle again it will be in different circumstances, with different people and with a more positive attitude on my part. I will then be able to find the *real* story of the Pendle witches.

Pendle in Lancashire is of course not the only place where I have come up against the spirit entities of people who have practised witchcraft during their physical lives. Everywhere in the British Isles has had a history of witchcraft at some point. I have come into contact with many of these witches. Some of these have been pleasant experiences and some have not been so pleasant. The one that stands out as the worst took place in Essex.

The Essex marshes themselves are in places desolate, and in winter cold and damp. The mists swirl through wooded areas and conjure up pictures of hobgoblins

and elves. There is a 'feel' about the place that is mysterious and unsettling. One could easily imagine the
marshes being the backdrop for a Dennis Wheatley
horror story.

I had been asked to conduct an investigation at the
home of Tania and Earl, which lay on the edge of the
Essex marshes. For some time this couple had been
experiencing some rather unsettling goings-on.

It was a dark winter's evening when Ray and I
arrived at the door of Heron House. We both shuddered as we climbed out of the vehicle and hurried up
the path to the front door. It was opened by Tania, who
showed us through to the warmth of the sitting room.

Heron House, Tania told me, was around 200 years
old. It had been built by a local engineer. After experiencing the strange and sometimes frightening things
that happened in the house, both Tania and Earl had
traced back the history of the building. Their interest in
the paranormal had taught them that sometimes the
history of a house could hold the answers to certain
mysteries. They had friends who were also interested in
the subject. Together with these friends and the help of
a local medium, they had held a séance in order to
attempt to contact the spirit person responsible for the

disturbances. Tania assured me that the séance had been conducted properly in that adequate protection had been requested before it took place and that it had been concluded and closed properly according to accepted guidelines. I had no reason to disbelieve what she told me.

Earl continued by telling me that a person had been contacted during that séance, a spirit man by the name of Edward Johns who had at one time lived in the house but who seemed to be a benign and friendly chap. I accepted this fact because although I had not received a name, when walking into the room I had detected the spirit presence of a man who displayed a friendly and happy demeanour.

I asked Tania and Earl to tell me what had caused them to get in touch with me, especially as they had already contacted a medium with whom they seemed perfectly happy. They told me that the medium concerned had not wanted to delve any deeper into the reason behind what was going on in the house because she did not feel that she had the strength. I was more than pleased to hear that the lady concerned had shown great responsibility and had recognized that she would do more harm than good if she had attempted to take on a situation that was beyond her capabilities. In some situations not only is great spiritual strength a necessity for investigative mediums but physical strength is also needed to withstand the rigours to which they are occasionally subjected.

Earl told me that they had experienced very many inexplicable incidents in the house. Pictures would suddenly fall from their hangings, photographs would be knocked over, they would hear screams and screeches and an obnoxious smell would sometimes pervade the house – almost what they imagined burning flesh would smell like. The heating would suddenly turn itself off for no reason, causing the temperature in the house to fall, but it would fall so dramatically that it could not only be caused by the natural cooling down of the building. Earl was actually a central heating engineer and in spite of a thorough overhaul of the system, he could find nothing to explain this phenomenon.

I asked whether these events took place every day, every week or every month and whether there was a pattern or whether they happened randomly. Tania and Earl answered together. They had noticed that activity occurred throughout the year but January, May, July and November were strangely quiet. In other months the activity was heightened, especially on the nights of Hallowe'en and 30 April. I was immediately alerted to the fact that witchcraft might be involved, as I knew there were eight Sabbats, or festivals, on a witch's calendar, Samhain on 31 October and Beltane on 30 April being the most important. The remaining six were in December, February, March, June, August and September. I suspected, however, that what Tania and Earl were experiencing had nothing to do with the quiet following of the seasonal festivals celebrated by most witches. I suspected that there was something more sinister going on here.

To my knowledge, witches do not worship a devil. Their beliefs are very much the same as mine in that they do not believe in an evil being but more in the evil perpetrated by man. Their 'magic' is neutral, neither black nor white, but may be used either positively or negatively. It is obvious that the term 'black magic' refers to its negative use. It was my suspicion that negative or black magic had been practised by somebody who had at some time dwelt if not in Heron House then on the land upon which it was built.

I asked the couple if they had managed to find out whether anything had been on the land prior to the building of Heron House. Earl told me that two work-ers' cottages had once stood on the same spot.

It was time to take a walk around the house in the company of Tania, Earl and Ray. I sensed spirit activity in a bedroom – there was the spirit form of an elderly woman who nodded and smiled at me but was benign in nature. A young boy from the spirit world laughed and danced as he skittered along the landing on the first floor. The spectral outline of a black-and-white cat wound itself around the legs of a chair in the kitchen. The Edward Johns sensed by the medium who had visited prior to me did not make an appearance. Everything seemed calm and peaceful, although I could pick up an underlying 'something' – something that made the hairs at the back of my neck stand up.

'It's early yet,' Earl commented when I informed him of my findings. 'Things usually start happening around 10 o'clock at night.'

I looked at the clock. It was almost 9 p.m. An hour to wait!

The four of us sat in Tania and Earl's sitting room drinking coffee. I was pleased to learn how interested the couple were in my work. They had been avid followers of it since my days on Granada Breeze. They were intelligent people who asked relevant questions and who had not accepted blindly that the happenings in their home were paranormal. Each one had been carefully evaluated before being categorized as 'unexplainable'.

It was just after 10 o'clock when the first small sounds were noted by Ray. He was sitting in the chair nearest the door to the hallway. 'I think we've got company,' he told me.

We all sat and listened. The sound of shuffling could be heard coming from the hallway followed by a loud knocking noise which lasted for around 15 seconds. I rose from my chair and went over to the door, opening it suddenly. The noises immediately stopped. As I looked down the dimly lit hallway, a picture suddenly dropped from the wall, landing on the floor face down. Fortunately it was not glazed.

'We don't have any pictures covered in glass because this happens all the time,' Earl commented.

I walked out into the hallway, closely followed by Ray and Earl, with Tania following behind, and opened myself up fully to the atmosphere. As I became more and more aware, I was revolted by the emanations that swirled around me. I couldn't see anybody there, but could sense the sort of person that they had been. It was a person I would never wish to meet in life.

I could hear more noises in the kitchen so was heading in that direction when we were all brought to a sudden halt by a crash from the room in which we had been sitting. We all raced back to find that a companion set in the fireplace had crashed to its side on the marble hearth, the brass brush and shovel lying a couple of feet away on the carpet.

Now there were more noises from the hallway, moving towards the kitchen area. We went back through the sitting-room door and headed back into the kitchen. It was almost as though we were being lured into that room.

I stood by the kitchen table, rested my hands on its surface and demanded, 'Show yourself! Tell me who you are!'

In response, a low growling sound could be heard by all. Clairaudiently, I heard a man's voice shout, 'Never will you be rid of me! Never!' I knew at that moment that what I was dealing with was no ordinary spirit person but something far more malevolent than I had met before.

The spirit form of a man was building up in front of me. He was of medium height and build and dressed quite smartly in slim-fitting trousers with a short jacket and a white stiff-collared shirt. This ensemble was covered by a dark cloak. He wore a tall hat on his head and looked very much like the old-fashioned magicians that used to give shows at the seaside. The expression on the man's face, however, was pure evil. He stared at me coldly.

'Ha! Derek Acorah! And what do you think you can do?' he asked in a patronizing voice. 'Begone from here, you little man. You have nothing. You have no power. You *are* nothing!'

'What is your name?' I asked him in a low voice.

'You're so clever, you tell me!' he replied.

I had never been in a situation such as this before, but I knew that Sam was beside me – I could feel the warmth and lightness of his spirit. I could also feel the strength and power of my own guardians and gate-keepers, together with those of Tania, Earl and Ray.

Suddenly the man in spirit faded and disappeared, but I knew that he was still present. I felt a tremendous urge to go out into the back garden. We all donned our coats and, armed with torches, walked outside.

✳ ✳ ✳

I stood in the centre of the garden and looked around me. The mists from the marshes were swirling around and it was bitterly cold. I carefully shone the torch I was holding into all four corners of the garden. I then switched it off in order to accustom my eyes to the darkness.

After a moment or two my attention was drawn to movement around 20 feet away from me. It was a group of people – spirit people. They were standing around what looked like a square stone and were quietly chanting. Then the spirit form of another person walked through and laid a bundle on top of the square. The wrappings from the bundle were removed and a small baby was uncovered. The spirit man I had seen in the kitchen appeared, this time attired in a long black robe. He stared down at the child and then raised his arms above his head. In his clenched hands I could see the blade of a knife. I realized that I was witnessing the replay of a child sacrifice.

'Nooo!' I shouted out. I knew that the sacrifice was not taking place in reality, but I couldn't stop myself.

As my cry echoed in the air, the picture disappeared. I felt shaken by what I had seen. I now knew that what I was dealing with was witchcraft, negative witchcraft – in other words black magic!

'Are you alright, Derek?' Ray asked me. I told him that I was, but that I wanted to go back to the house.

Back in the kitchen the three of us sat around the table and I told Tania, Earl and Ray what I had seen.

'My God! How awful!' Tania said. 'D'you think that sacrifices took place here in this house?'

I told her that I thought not. It was my opinion that the land upon which Heron House had been built had been the site of rituals many long years ago, but I was sure that nothing had actually taken place in the building that now stood there.

'For you to live a happy and untroubled life here we have to get rid of the energies and evil spirit presences that visit from time to time,' I added.

Once more I went out in to the garden, instructing Tania and Earl to keep a distance from me and the area of the garden in which I was standing. I knew that Ray was well aware of what might happen and would be at hand should I need him.

I headed over to the part of the garden in which I had seen the awful re-enactment take place and stood on the very spot where the stone altar had been placed.

I very quickly became aware of spirit presence around me. The man I had first seen in the kitchen and whom I now recognized as the head of the group appeared before me. He seemed taller and larger than he had previously, but I knew very well that this was how he wanted to appear to me. He wanted me to feel threatened and vulnerable.

I began to feel a sensation of being closed in – of people coming closer and closer to me. I felt as though I was being buffeted and pressed. I could hear a loud chanting in my ears and my head began to pound. I desperately hung on to my senses, but the power of the spirit people and their negativity were beginning to tell on me. I could hear Ray's voice shouting my name and I tried vainly to reply to him. I knew that my only salvation was Sam and my guardians and gatekeepers. I tried desperately to concentrate on my spirit guide – on his goodness and light. I prayed as I had never prayed before.

Then I felt myself being half-dragged and half-carried – it was Ray who, recognizing the difficulty that I was in, knew that he must get me away from the immediate vicinity. Thank goodness that he had been with me long enough to recognize the point at which I had to be removed from a situation.

I was unceremoniously dumped against the wall of the house. 'Derek! Derek!' I heard Ray shouting at me urgently. 'Come on, Derek!' he repeated over and over again.

I gradually began to gather my wits and to look around me. The garden was clear – I could see nothing – but I knew that the evil spirits were still lingering, waiting to pounce and continue their satanic ways. I got to my feet.

Sam spoke. 'You and your companions have to help us, Derek,' he said. 'We can do what we can from this side, but we need a little help from you. The area must be cleansed in order to prevent these spirits from ever returning to this place.'

I knew what I had to do. I asked Earl and Tania whether they would agree to take part in a cleansing ritual in order to rid the whole of the area of the evil emanations. They readily agreed.

The four of us sat around the kitchen table. I prayed to the spirit world and asked that not only Sam, my own spirit guide, but all my gatekeepers and the guides and guardians of Tania, Earl and Ray might gather together in order to overcome the evil presence that was attempting to take over the beautiful Heron House. As

I closed my eyes and continued my fervent pleas I clair-voyantly saw the black images slowly melt and disap-pear, to be replaced by pure white light and positive energy. I knew then that Tania and Earl would be both-ered no more.

It is rare that evil forces join together, but it certainly does happen and this was one of those occasions. I hope that I never have to experience again what I went through that night in Essex.

Chapter Fourteen

Civil War in a Public House

The ancient city of Chester has been a place I have loved to visit since my childhood. In those long-ago days it was not the ancient Tudor buildings and the architecture that held me in thrall, as history was one of my least favourite subjects and to be avoided at all costs, but rather the visits to the zoo and the boat trips along the river Dee. These trips afforded the opportunity for a spot of fishing. With a net and a deft hand, I could fill a jam jar with tiddlers prior to tea at one of the riverside cafés or a picnic with my brothers and sisters on the bank of the river. Later, in my late teens, Chester was a place to visit for a night out.

It has only been in latter years, perhaps the last 20 or so, that I have begun to appreciate Chester for what it is

– a beautiful old city full of reminders of its ancient history. I have walked the Roman city walls and wondered at the monumental effort entailed in building such a structure without today's modern machinery. I have toured the streets with their original Tudor and Stuart black-and-white buildings. The framework of many of the original buildings in Chester is constructed from the Spanish oak taken from the ribs of the ships that ended their days in the port of Chester in the seventeenth century. The notches in the beams of these old buildings where wooden pegs were used to hold the ships together are testament to this fact.

Stories of hauntings in Chester are legion. There are numerous reports of ghosts in the city and a plethora of people willing to come forward to tell how they met up with a local ghost. It was such a story, related to me by somebody who had visited a public house in Chester, that whetted my appetite enough to go along and see for myself.

The Boot Inn is in Eastgate Row. Built in 1643, it is purported to be one of the oldest buildings in Chester. Access to it is gained by climbing a narrow staircase from street level up to the row above. Anybody familiar with the streets of Chester will know that in a number of them there are not only the street-level retail outlets but also a row above, which can be reached by narrow sets of stone steps. You may then walk along the covered walkways – wonderful in inclement weather.

I walked along the ramparts and opened the door to the Boot Inn. Immediately I entered the old public house my senses were assailed by massed levels of residual energy. In a building of this age, with all the activity that had taken place within its walls over the centuries, it would be inevitable that I would sense many layers of energy, of spirit activity and presence.

I walked through the long front bar room, which was curiously bare of the usual brass ornaments and trappings one expects to see in old public houses. There were no polished horse brasses on the bar stanchions, no pewter vases and no bucolic prints on the walls. It was quite a dark and austere place in fact, with just the ordinary public-house tables and stools to be seen everywhere in hostelries throughout the land. To describe it as being 'nondescript' would be unfair, though, because the Boot Inn had a presence of its own – something not often found in the other busy inns that I have visited.

There were only one or two customers sitting at tables at the time of my visit, which was towards closing time. They showed no interest in me whatsoever as I walked through their midst, but were more interested in finishing their drinks and finding their way home.

By 11.30 p.m. the place was empty and quiet. I sat down in the main bar and concentrated on what I was receiving through my psychic senses. The name 'John' came into my mind and I gained the impression of a jovial man. As I sat there concentrating, a picture built up of a man who was no stranger to hard work and to dealing with the odd recalcitrant customer who had imbibed of the publican's hospitality a little over much.

'This was mine!' I heard a voice say. I shifted my gaze to a place near the bar, and as I watched, the spirit of the very man I had seen in my mind's eye built up before me. He was around 5 ft 8 inches in height and of strong build. His hair was thinning but he was the owner of a very impressive set of whiskers. For some reason I gained the impression that his hospitality had gone beyond that of most landlords in that he seemed to be offering me a 'wash and brush up' and a 'good close shave'. He was beaming at me, his round face and twinkling eyes giving me the impression that in his time he had been a popular landlord.

Moments later he was joined by a woman in spirit. She was of ample proportions and it was obvious that she was proud of the fare that she offered to her clients. Then I heard a loud 'tut'! 'They were not clients, they were friends!' she conveyed to me. 'People used to return again and again for a taste of my good roast beef!'

I silently apologized to the spirit lady, who was bristling with indignation. As I did so, I heard a chuckle at my side. 'That'll teach you,' I heard Sam's amused voice say.

I opened myself up further to the emanations of the old pub. It had been a very busy place at one time. Lots of bartering and bargaining had taken place within its walls – in more ways than one! I heard the sound of horses' hooves and the jingling of harness outside in the street below. Pictures unfolded to my clairvoyant eye – pictures of groups of men deep in discussion. I knew that these discussions involved deals in horseflesh.

I moved away from where I was sitting and proceeded up the stairs that were located towards the front of the room. Halfway up the staircase there was an area laid bare of plaster to exhibit the original structure of the old building. The wattle and daub, stark in its simplicity, put to shame the modern building materials of concrete and breeze block.

At the top of the stairs was a room marked 'Eastgate Room'. As I entered the darkly panelled room resplendent with a large fireplace I gained the impression of gentlemen dining elegantly on the offerings of the proud landlady. These were indeed gentlemen and not of the type of people who inhabited the lower floor. They were men of means, involved in the running and commerce of the city of Chester – men not to be trifled with. As I entered the room and closed the door behind me, one such gentleman stood up in acknowledgement of my presence. He bowed and gestured towards a chair. The atmosphere was one of calm and comfort and good living – far removed from the difficulties and hardships suffered by some in those harsh nineteenth-century days.

I retreated from the room and walked a little further along the corridor. Another door bore the words 'Ladies' and 'Gents' – the toilet facilities for the public house's modern-day clients. I opened the door and was not surprised to see that to my clairvoyant eye all signs of porcelain bathroom paraphernalia disappeared, to be replaced by plain bedrooms, obviously there to accommodate overnight travellers visiting Chester or passing through the city.

I became aware of a young serving girl dressed in plain calico. She was totally unaware of my presence as she scurried along, going about her business of cleaning the rooms ready for the next customer.

I went back down the stairs. What I found strange was the fact that up to that point in time, apart from the serving girl and the landlady, I had sensed no female presence in the public house for that level of time. Then, as I reached an area of the main bar, I realized why I had not seen any ladies taking coffee or tea, for ranged along a bench were the ghostly forms of Victorian 'ladies of the night' – there to sell their services to travellers and perhaps to one of the gentlemen after he had enjoyed his dinner in the upstairs dining room.

I reached the main bar area and walked past the bar itself then into the second main section of the public house. Through this bar I came to a smaller flagstoned room. Here I could hear whisperings and intrigue. It

was though I had been whisked back further in time –
to the mid-seventeenth century, not long after the old
pub had been built. The picture that unfolded before
my eyes was of men garbed in the flamboyant dress of
cavaliers. Their feathered headgear, silks and satins
glistened in the ghostly firelight. Candles on tables illuminated the scene. It was like looking at a painting of
times gone by, but here I could sense the heavy reality of
fear.

Suddenly the door burst open and in stormed a
number of men dressed in the stark plain uniform of
Cromwellian soldiers. The sound of gunshots rang out.
Mayhem reigned. Immediately I felt the great sense of
hopelessness that can arise with the knowledge of
imminent death. I could hear screams of pain and the
names of loved ones being shouted out. The stench of
flowing blood assailed my nostrils, together with the
acrid smell of gunpowder.

A searing pain shot through my stomach and I staggered backwards. It was almost as though I had been
shot myself. I was in absolute agony. I knew that I was
channelling the last moments of a man who had
been almost disembowelled by gunshot. I groaned
involuntarily, such was the pain I was experiencing. I

211

desperately clung on to my senses and focused on the wall in front of me. 'Don't let go, Derek! Don't let go!' I told myself. My hands clutching at my stomach and abdomen, I exerted all my willpower to overcome what I was experiencing through my psychic senses. I broke out into a cold sweat, such was the effort I was making. I had only ever experienced this depth of agony when I had visited battlegrounds where men had been ripped asunder by guns.

I realized that I had fallen to my knees and was trying to crawl away from the scene to get myself away from the depth of emotion contained in the residual energy of the ancient walls. With a monumental effort, I managed to get myself far enough away from the scene of the awful event. Slowly, slowly, the agonies I was experiencing began to recede and as I concentrated on the present-day room I began to get a grip on reality once more. Gradually the scene and the sounds of the past began to fade. I lay where I was, exhausted by my experiences.

As I slowly began to recover, I was able to look at the situation in a calmer manner. I was interested to note that amongst all the mayhem and agony that had taken place, I had sensed the presence of guides and helpers waiting to help the poor suffering men over to the world of spirit. Again, this was something that I had never experienced before. I had certainly picked up the energies of those present at a battle before, but never before had I relived a scene in enough detail to witness this phenomenon.

I felt totally drained by my experiences in that room of the old public house and decided to discontinue the investigation. But I would like to revisit the premises at some time in the future to delve further into the hundreds of years of history contained in its four walls. I don't think that I will be disappointed.

CHAPTER FIFTEEN

The Haunted Hotel

Sitting at the foot of a slope and looking out over Torquay Bay, this hotel is one of the best known and frequented in a town full of hotels, guest houses and B&Bs. The beautiful old building is a delight to stay in for a night or two.

Of course the visitors are not all of the worldly type, for there are ghosts aplenty walking the long corridors of the lovely old hotel. The building is very large, having been extended on more than one occasion, and the hotel has well over 100 bedrooms, together with function rooms, dining rooms, a library, conservatory and bar.

During World War II the cellars of the hotel, now housing the swimming pool, used to be a major public air-raid shelter. It is the echoes of those long-gone days that come back from time to time. A conversation between two women, one named Elspeth, has been heard on numerous occasions.

As in the case of any hotel, large or small, there have been a number of passings to spirit from the premises during its long history. None was more tragic than the occasion some years ago when a young man in his late twenties booked in for a night. He showed no signs of distress upon his arrival, but the following morning his body was found hanging from the bathroom door. His family in Plymouth were contacted and it was discovered that he had experienced some problems at his workplace. Unable to cope, he had decided to end his physical life in room 112.

Some weeks after this tragic incident a man was booked into that very room. The following morning he approached the staff at reception and asked whether anybody had died in the room in which he had been staying, because all night he had experienced a feeling of not being alone. 'I could feel a presence in there,' he told the astounded staff.

Room 221 was the scene of another tragic suicide. To this day the identity of the young Asian man remains a mystery, though it is thought that he travelled to the UK as a worker for the Tamil Tigers. His mission was unsuccessful, so rather than return to his own country to face his fate, he took matters into his own hands in room 221. Ever the gentleman, he left the money for his dinner on the dressing table of the bedroom. He did not want to enter the spirit world with a debt on his conscience.

The ghostly presences of these two young men have both been seen on the first and second floors of the hotel.

Spirits have also been seen in the reception area. There is a large mirror here and staff have reported seeing the reflection of a man in it when no man has been physically present.

Perhaps the most horrible of ghosts is that which is said to inhabit the corridors of the third floor, particularly room 305.

A husband and wife were once staying there for the night and had retired to bed. After switching off the light, the man was just about to drift off to sleep when he became aware of the dark shadowy figure of a man standing at the foot of the bed. To his horror, it began to move up the bed towards him. As it drew closer, he felt hands go around his throat and the dark face was replaced by a hooded skeletal visage. His cries for help woke his wife, who immediately switched on the light. To their horror, they could see bruising in the shape of thumbprints on the man's neck.

The following morning the couple booked out of the hotel. 'Did you have a good night's sleep?' they were asked. 'No we did not!' came the sharp reply and the unhappy couple related the strange and frightening events that had taken place the night before. 'And d'you know,' the man said, 'I just know that there is a painting of the man I saw last night somewhere in this hotel!'

The manager told him that as far as he was aware there was only one such painting in the hotel and he walked the couple through to the dining room to view it.

As soon as the man saw it, he cried, 'That's it! That's it! He's a lot younger in the painting – in fact he's just a lad – but it's the same person!'

The painting was that of Sir John Gordon Watson, 1790–1864.

* * *

Each year I travel to Torquay to appear at the Princess Theatre on the sea front there. I had stayed in the hotel previously and had been regaled with stories of its ghostly history by one of the staff, but 12 months later, with many theatre shows and much ghost hunting having taken place in the meantime, I had completely forgotten these tales when I was shown to room 305 by the porter. Ray was booked into the room next door to mine.

After the show we arrived back at the hotel, sat in the lounge bar with some sandwiches and tea and eventually retired to bed not long after one in the morning. It is always our practice to relax and wind down after a show in this manner.

I was tired and after a quick shower I jumped into bed, turned out the light and fell asleep almost immediately.

Suddenly I woke up. The room was in total darkness, due to the heavy curtains across the windows. I strained my eyes peering fruitlessly into the darkness.

Then I heard a noise. It was a clicking sound, almost like a door being shut. I heard a shuffling noise, followed by definitive footsteps moving around the room. I switched on the bedside light. At once all sound ceased.

No one was there. I couldn't see any spiritual activity in the room either, or feel anything clairsentiently.

I looked at my watch and noted that it was almost three o'clock in the morning. I had been asleep for at least an hour and a half. I got up out of bed and opened the curtains a little before returning to bed and getting under the covers. I switched off the light and settled back down to sleep.

After a few moments I once again heard the shuffling noise and the footsteps, this time nearer the bed. I opened my eyes.

In the dim light I could make out the spirit form of a man. He was standing at the foot of my bed and although I could not see his face, I was aware that he was staring down at me.

The room was growing colder and colder and I felt my heart clench with sudden fright. I was not ready for this. I had done a hard evening's work and felt physically and psychically drained. Hastily I called upon Sam and whispered my prayer, the one I always use prior to investigations.

After a few moments I felt an enormous surge of energy and before I knew it the spirit man was launching himself at me, arms outstretched towards my throat. I automatically threw up my hands in defence, but they ineffectually beat out against nothing. The pressure on my neck was enormous and I almost felt as though my eyes were bulging out of their sockets. The intense pressure continued, then suddenly the dark masculine shape seemed to be illuminated from behind and I felt the power of goodness and love surround me and the evil entity that was attacking me. The pressure on my throat and neck relaxed and I slumped back onto my pillows. What little strength I had left drained from me completely and I doubted that I would have sufficient energy to withstand a further attack. However, I knew that Sam was an exceedingly powerful spirit and that it was his energy, together with that of my other spiritual protectors, that had manifested in the light of goodness – it was they who were repelling the spirit man by surrounding him and pushing him back to the place from where he had come.

Gradually the light diminished and the atmosphere in the hotel bedroom returned to its previous calm and anonymity. Exhausted, I fell asleep.

The following morning I awoke to the sound of Ray knocking on my door. 'Come on, Derek! Get up!' he shouted.

I got out of bed and opened the door.

'Good God, man! What've you been doing?' he asked as he saw my haggard face.

I proceeded to tell him about the events that had taken place.

'Are you sure it wasn't just a nightmare?' he asked me.

I knew that this had not been the case. I knew the difference between dreams and reality and what had happened to me had been terribly real. I was determined to find out more about the reason for it.

Ray and I spent the day relaxing, wandering around Torquay's town centre and generally killing time until I was due at the theatre for the second night's demonstration. I had discussed the previous night's events with Ray and had decided that the only way to discover what was going on in room 305 was to invoke the spirit of the man who had attacked me the previous night.

'I'll come into your room while you do it,' Ray responded. 'I'm not having you on your own for this.'

So that night, after we had returned to the hotel and had our late supper, we both went to my room. All was quiet and peaceful and there was nothing untoward with regard to the atmosphere.

I lay on the bed and Ray settled into an armchair by the window. I closed my eyes and began to ask quietly for the spirit man to show himself.

Nothing happened.

Time and again I whispered my request. Still nothing.

By now I could hear Ray breathing steadily and evenly in the chair and knew that he had dropped off to sleep. I must have fallen into a light doze myself, because the next thing I was awakened by the same clicking noise that I had heard the night before. There was movement in the room. Swirls of cold air were flowing over me and although I could see nothing clairvoyantly, I knew that there was spirit presence in the room.

I shuddered as the temperature dropped even further. Then gradually I began to make out the outline of the same man that I had seen the night before. It grew and solidified as it seemed to hover at the end of the bed.

Once more I was aware of Sam's presence by my side. 'You must help this soul,' I heard him tell me. 'He is not evil, but he is lost. George needs your help.'

I was astounded. I did not understand how a spirit who had flown at my throat and tried to throttle me the night before could not be considered to be bad. On reflection, though, I did not recall picking up evil emanations from the man prior to his attack upon me.

Sam then told George's story. He had been born with a health problem that had resulted in his mental age never exceeding that of a young child of around eight or nine. In the early Victorian era people were ashamed of such afflictions and usually sent any family member thus affected away to an institution where they would spend their days hidden away from the world. In George's case his family had not wanted to do this, but still could not bring themselves to allow him to be seen in public. So whenever they travelled away from home they would keep George locked in their hotel room.

On one occasion when the family had been visiting Torquay and George had been locked in the hotel room, a porter had had cause to make a delivery to the room. On finding George on his own he had begun to taunt the poor man, laughing at him and generally making fun of him. This treatment had resulted in George becoming so hysterical that he had collapsed with a seizure. On seeing him fall to the floor, the porter had fled and had said not a word to anybody.

The family had returned to the hotel room later to find that as a result of the seizure George had suffered a massive heart attack and had passed on to the world of spirit.

From that day onward George's spirit had remained in the hotel, afraid to move on and afraid of any man who entered the room. For the majority of the time he would remain quiet and unseen by the ever-changing occupants of the room, but on occasion his spirit would recall the vicious taunting and he would attack any man who happened to be in the room at the time.

Now George's dark shadow was again at the end of my bed. Again there was a sudden powerful lunge and the outstretched arms reached out for my throat.

This time I was ready! I rolled to my side and leaped quickly from the bed.

The thud of my feet on the floor wakened Ray. 'What's going on?' he whispered loudly.

'Stay where you are, Ray – don't move!' I told him urgently.

I began by demanding that George's guides and guardians come to help the lost soul. I prayed to God and the goodness of the world of spirit to help him. I could see him standing next to the bed looking lost and hurt, all thoughts of attacking me now gone. I pleaded with his family in spirit to come to the room to collect him – to take him with them to the heavenly state where he could recuperate and become whole both physically and mentally.

A glimmer of light began to appear in the vicinity of where George was standing. It grew and grew until it formed the outline of a lady. She was dressed in a long Victorian-style gown and had a beautiful smile on her face. She reached out her hand to George. He looked down at her and his features melted into a smile of recognition.

'George's mother, Elizabeth,' Sam told me quietly.

'Please take your son, Elizabeth. Please take him to join you and the rest of his family,' I prayed to her.

The light surrounding the spirit woman grew and expanded to encompass another, older woman from the spirit world – George's grandmother, come to help his mother to guide his footsteps to the heavenly side of life.

Then white light seemed to surround George. Gradually he faded and was absorbed into the glow, which then began to recede and finally disappeared.

Now there was peace and calm in the room. I felt jubilant that George was at peace with his family at last.

No more would that frightened man's spirit relive the horrors of his life whilst here in the physical world.

Ray and I made a cup of tea before he went off to his own room. Whilst we drank it I told him the story of poor George. He asked about the hooded skeletal-faced figure experienced by one of the previous occupants of the room.

'The man was mistaken,' I told Ray. 'His recall of what had happened had become blurred and exaggerated. There was definitely nothing active in the room apart from George, who certainly did not fit that description. And he didn't look like the painting of Sir John in the dining room either.'

I have noted over the years that this is a common occurrence. A person may see a spirit, but may describe a painting or a photograph of someone entirely different. The man who had reported being attacked in room 305 had been to dinner with his wife before retiring and had obviously been struck by the painting of Sir John that was hanging in the dining room. When woken suddenly by the attack by George, who was similarly dressed but obviously younger, he had assumed that it was the same person when in fact it was not.

* * *

The following morning Ray and I booked out of the hotel.

'Did you have a good night, sir?' asked the receptionist.

'Yes, thank you – eventually!' I replied.

CHAPTER SIXTEEN

The Green-eyed Monster

Blackpool is a Lancashire town that I have been visiting since childhood. I still remember fondly the days of candy floss and donkey rides on the beach during hot summers and the awe-inspiring 'chara' trips to see the lights once the chilly autumn days had come around. I used to look forward to seeing the lights, but even more to the fish and chip suppers eaten out of newspapers whilst walking along the sea front.

Now of course those newspaper-wrapped delights are no more, but I still enjoy my visits to Blackpool when I appear at the Grand Theatre each year. It was during one such visit that I was asked to take part in an investigation of a private house.

* * *

Jane and Tony had lived in Blackpool all their lives. They were in their late twenties when I met them and were the owners of a large three-storey house near the centre of the town. Jane had always been interested in spiritual matters, but that interest had grown over the years and she was now a regular visitor to her local Spiritualist church. She had seen me work when I had been the visiting medium many years earlier at the Morecambe Spiritualist church and I was flattered when she told me that she had not been surprised when she turned on the television one day and tuned in to Granada Breeze's *Psychic Livetime* programme. 'I always knew that you'd do well, Derek,' she said. 'I've never forgotten that evening in Morecambe. You inspired me to develop my own psychic abilities and now I'm sitting in a development circle.'

Upon meeting Jane I had known that she was very sensitive. I asked her why she had asked me to come along and investigate her home.

Jane and Tony sat and told me what had been happening. They had always thought that there was a presence in their home. Activity would manifest in different ways. Jane and Tony would notice that items had been moved around, especially in the kitchen area.

They would also hear movements around their home at night – footfalls on the staircase and shuffling sounds. They described one of the top-floor bedrooms as having a 'nasty feel' to it.

'I know that my own and Tony's family members in spirit visit us occasionally,' Jane told me, 'but this is different. This is something else. As my development has progressed, I can now sense something more than just family coming to call.'

After Jane and Tony had spoken to me for some time regarding their experiences in the house, it was time for them to take me on a walk around the different rooms. We started on the ground floor, which comprised a very large hallway, a living room, a sitting room, a dining room and a large kitchen.

As I walked around I became more and more of the opinion that this house had not always been a private home but had at one time been an establishment where people had come to stay. From the residual energy I sensed staff moving around carrying out their daily tasks and the general business of a hotel. I picked up the spirit presence of a porter in the hallway waiting patiently to carry the next guest's luggage up to a bedroom. He didn't seem at all bothered by the fact that the house had changed dramatically since his days working there. He stood smartly to attention in his livery, nodding and smiling every now and again at guests whose energies were obviously operating on his plane.

We moved on to the dining room. As soon as I walked through the door I received the name 'John' clairaudiently. 'John! John! John!' The name resounded around the room. I got the impression of a man who frequently showed signs of temper. I walked slowly around the room, absorbing the atmosphere and asking this 'John' to show himself.

After a few minutes, the spirit form of a man gradually began to build. He was of average build and height and looked to me to be between 40 and 50 years of age. He had dark hair and a noticeable dark moustache. His attire did not appear appropriate for a dining room in that he was rather roughly dressed in heavy trousers, rolled-up shirtsleeves and a waistcoat. He simply stood there and stared at me impassively.

'You're John?' I asked.

He merely replied with a nod. Then his features suddenly darkened into a scowl. He strode towards the door leading to the hallway and then evaporated into the ether.

I was intrigued. I had sensed that John was not a particularly even-tempered man – the emanations of his ill humour had been evident even before he showed himself in spirit – but I was more than interested in what had brought about the sudden change in his expression.

I asked Jane whether she had picked up anything from the atmosphere of the room. 'I didn't feel very comfortable for a few moments, Derek,' she replied. 'I felt that somebody was spoiling for a fight, but I couldn't pick up or understand why or with whom.'

She went on to tell me that very occasionally she had sensed a similar feeling in the dining room – an aggression in the atmosphere – but that she had never experienced the manifestation of a spirit entity.

We moved out of the dining room and headed in the direction of the kitchen. I was amazed at the size of the room with its enormous Aga filling the alcove of one wall.

'That's where the old kitchen range used to be situated,' Tony told me.

I had no need to be given such information because very soon after I had walked through the door, the whole room had transformed and I had found myself transported back to a Victorian kitchen with a huge black range with a couple of well-cushioned rocking chairs in front of it. There was a large well-scrubbed kitchen table and lots of pans and coppers ranged along the top of the cupboards and hanging from the wall. The smell of baking wafted through the air and I had the impression of a plump woman in a cook's apron and cap busily kneading something in a basin at the table. 'Sarah,' a discarnate voice told me.

After this glimpse of the 'what was', I was rapidly transported back to the 'what is' and the present-day kitchen. Again I walked around the room absorbing the atmosphere. I stopped at the part of the worktop that contained a number of drawers.

'Are there knives in these drawers?' I asked Jane.

'There are,' she confirmed, 'and it is those drawers and the carving knives in them that we find are interfered with most.'

I was beginning to build up a picture. But just as Jane was about to tell me something more, the spirit form of John once more began to materialize. He still wore his ill-humoured expression and seemed to position himself near the drawer with the large knives.

I felt that there was a very strong connection between John and Sarah. I also sensed that there was a sadness lying between them, but it was a sadness born of unrest and argument, of threats and violence.

We left the kitchen and walked through the sitting room and the room which Tony and Jane used as a general living area. As we did so, Jane told me about the various spirit presences she had picked up on during her time in the house. Some of the emanations were very prevalent whilst I was walking around with her, but others were not so evident.

We finally began to mount the stairs to the first floor of the building. After visiting two or three of the bedrooms, which, although they contained lots of residual energy, showed no sign of any particular spirit activity, I suggested that we move on to the second floor.

As soon as I placed my first foot on the staircase to the second floor that I knew that we would experience spirit activity there. I also knew that something untoward had taken place in one of the bedrooms at the top of the house. As we climbed the stairs, these feelings became stronger and stronger.

Up on the second floor I did not wait to be shown from bedroom to bedroom but headed straight for a door halfway along the landing. As I neared it I became aware of the sounds of harsh words from a man, a woman crying and a fist landing on flesh.

I stood with Jane outside the door and asked her whether she could hear anything. She shook her head, but shuddered. 'I just knew that you'd be led to this bedroom,' she told me. 'This is the bedroom we told you about earlier – the one with the horrible nasty feel to it!'

I opened the door. The room was carpeted, though there was very little furniture in it. It contained just a simple single bed and a small bedside cabinet.

'We don't really use these rooms up here,' Tony commented. 'It's just emergency bedroom space really, in case we have a large family gathering. Most of the rooms up here are empty at the moment because we haven't got around to furnishing them.'

I was almost oblivious to what Tony was telling me. My senses were concentrated on the emanations I was picking up from the residual energy of the room. It was not a nice atmosphere at all. I sensed harsh words and physical violence.

Once more the spirit of John began to build up. As his ethereal outline solidified I noted with horror that in his hand he held a knife. His face was contorted with anger as he was staring down at the floor. My eyes followed his and I was horrified to see the vague form of a woman lying on what appeared to be bare boards. It was Sarah. She was dressed only in a light shift. She lay in a large pool of blood – her throat had been cut from ear to ear. There were signs of bruising on her bare arms. Her eyes were open and although all life had left her, they seemed to hold an expression of horrified panic.

The picture of the woman faded and I looked up at the more solid spirit form of John. For the first time he spoke. 'She deserved it!' he sneered. 'She was always up to her tricks, meeting other men behind my back and then acting as though she was innocent. I was tired of her ways, but nobody was going to have her if I couldn't. Lucy and May knew what she was up to, but they covered up for her.'

I realized that this man was literally mad with jealousy. From what I had picked up of Sarah's emanations she had been a decent clean-living woman who had had no time for anything other than her work and her family. She had been entirely innocent of what her husband was accusing her of. He had killed her with only his irrational paranoia as an excuse. What a waste of a life!

I turned to Jane and asked, 'Can you see him? Can you see the man in spirit who gives his name as John?'

Jane replied, 'I can see something, but it's not clear. I can feel his anger, though. I can feel that something really bad happened in this room, but I'm not sure what.'

I felt that it might be prudent to wait until we arrived back downstairs before I told Jane and Tony exactly what I had seen.

I turned to John. 'You have to move on,' I told him. 'You have to leave this home. You can't remain here. You must go to your designated place on the higher side of life.'

He stared at me long and hard, then seemed to shrug in a resigned manner. He looked at me once again and then, to my horror, simply started to disintegrate. He did not melt and fade in the manner of spirit people but seemed to decompose before my very eyes. I could even smell the stench of rotting flesh. His body seemed to collapse inwards and then liquefy before disappearing altogether. It was one of the most gruesome scenes I had ever witnessed.

The important thing, however, was that the atmosphere was clear of his presence and I knew that it would remain so. He had left this house forever. I had expected a struggle, but happily that had not happened.

I questioned Sam as to why John had been so accepting of his fate. Sam told me that he had been harshly brought up and this had resulted in an almost callous indifference towards other people. Nevertheless he had married Sarah and they had had two daughters together. As the years had gone by, however, John had become very suspicious of his wife and could not bear the thought of another man looking at her. She gave him no reason for his insane jealousy and bore his constant accusations quietly. As time progressed, he became violent and this had culminated in him murdering his wife. Realizing what he had done and having no care for anybody, John had committed suicide by walking into the sea and drowning himself. His spirit had returned to the home that he had shared with Sarah – the room on the third floor of the hotel in which they had both worked.

'He was sick of mind, Derek,' Sam explained. 'He has to atone for his sins, but his judgement will not be harsh.'

I related Sam's words to Jane and Tony.

'What a sad thing to happen,' Jane murmured. 'I feel very sorry for the poor woman, but I also feel a little sad for John. He must have loved Sarah – it was just that he was so jealous he ended up killing her because of it.'

I was sorry too. It was all so terribly unnecessary.

The three of us went back down to the ground floor. 'Thank you so much for helping us,' Jane and Tony said as I prepared to leave. 'You've answered a lot of questions for us.'

As I walked down their pathway I turned and waved. It was such a sad story, and the saddest part about it was that the house was such a lovely place. It was large and comfortable and would make a marvellous home for the family that I knew Jane and Tony would eventually have. My only concern was that Jane, through her sensitivity, would always be aware of the residual energy of the events that had taken place in that top-floor bedroom. I hoped that she would not venture up the stairs too often and that if she did, she would follow my advice to protect herself from the remnants of those energies.

It is unfortunate that you can move spirit entities on and can help them progress to the higher side of life, but you can never remove from the fabric of a building the memories of what has happened between the four walls.

CHAPTER SEVENTEEN

Spirit Children

It was April 2006 and I had been asked to assist the Anthony Nolan Trust to raise funds for their worthy cause of bone marrow donation by taking part in a 'Fright Night' at Chillingham Castle. I was more than happy to oblige. I had visited Chillingham two or three years earlier and had found it to be a fascinating place. The castle, lying deep in the Northumberland country-side, is reputed to be the most haunted in England and since the 1200s has been continuously owned by the family of Earls Grey and their descendants. It has changed little since the fourteenth century.

I drove along the bumpy driveway flanked by woods that gave way to a tall turreted wall. At the end of the wall was a sweeping circle of gravel that fronted the main entrance to the castle. I, however, was to drive to a small rear area where I would park my car and introduce myself to John, who was the representative of the Anthony Nolan Trust.

It began to rain as I climbed out of my car, but I was quickly shown to a room set aside for me to change into my 'working clothes' of black suit and sombre-coloured shirt. I would be appearing for two nights at Chillingham. First of all I would give a demonstration of mediumship in the courtyard. Then I would talk to the various groups of people who were conducting vigils at key points within the castle about their experiences during those vigils.

After changing my clothes I went through a rear doorway and walked along a corridor heading towards the Great Hall. As I entered this old and impressive room, dominated by its huge fireplace, I looked around me and once more absorbed the atmosphere of one of my favourite English castles. At the far end of the room there was a minstrels' gallery. On one wall long windows looked out over the courtyard; on the opposite wall monstrous and ancient elk antlers loomed large, unmissable in their grandeur. I reflected on the animal who would have been big enough to carry this amazing headgear around.

The hall was still and silent, as the people who were taking part in the night's proceedings had not yet entered the room. The spirits were, however, present. I could sense that they were all around me, just as they had been on my previous visit to Chillingham.

During my many years of investigations of haunted locations I have often met up with the spirits of long-gone children. Some are happy, some are confused and lost, some passed over to the world of spirit in anguish whilst others passed on to the life beyond serene and at peace. One of my saddest experiences communicating with a spirit child took place at Chillingham.

The Grey Room is located in the part of the castle that is inhabited by the present owner and his family. Consequently it is a pleasant warm bedroom containing furnishings I would describe as Victorian. It is a large room with a window looking out over the court-yard.

I entered the bedroom and walked towards the centre, where I stood still. I felt an overwhelming sensation of hurt and fear creeping up over me. I felt desolation and despair, fear and foreboding. As I was absorbing the energies that were making themselves evident to me I became aware of a small boy, eight or nine years of age. As he drew closer to me I knew that he wanted to tell me his story. I allowed him to come closer and closer and eventually to overshadow my being in order to communicate his story to me.

I was a young boy! I felt tears streaming down my face. 'Leave me alone!' I cried. 'Please leave me alone!'

The boy was not speaking to me — rather he was speaking through me. Travelling down through the years were his voice and his despair and hurt at the treatment meted out by the man he knew as his uncle.

'Sam,' I silently pleaded, 'take this off me.' As I stood there trembling, I felt the love and warmth of Sam permeate my body.

I opened my eyes and was once again in the warm bedroom. On the opposite wall I saw a doorway next to the fireplace. I felt inexplicably drawn to it. I needed to go through this doorway.

Beyond was another door, but it was the sections between the two doors to which I felt drawn. This was not the solid stone that formed the structure of the rest of the castle. I rapped on the walls with my knuckles and was greeted by a hollow response.

Then I saw the spirit of a young boy – the same boy who had so recently spoken through me. He was surrounded by a healing blue colour.

I was later told that the bones of a young boy and an adult man had been discovered in the very portion of the wall upon which I had been knocking. Scraps of blue material had been found with the bones. Many people visiting the castle have had sightings of the 'blue' or 'radiant' boy, as this spirit is known.

There have been many other occasions when I have investigated locations where the spirits of children have been evident. In the majority of cases these children are in visitation to the homes in which they lived when they were in their physical life here on Earth. These child spirits are happy to return and I do not feel the need to rid the atmosphere of their joy, as this can only have a beneficial effect on the homes their spirits occasionally inhabit.

There are some occasions, however, such as in the case of the 'blue boy' of Chillingham Castle, when rescue is necessary. On each and every occasion I do my best to send these poor lost children over to the light, back to their families in the spirit world where they can be nurtured and cared for.

The experiences of these children prior to their passing to spirit are sometimes horrendous. Susie's story is one that will live with me forever.

In the early 1990s I was called to a house on the outskirts of Liverpool city centre. It was a terraced house in one of the poorer districts, about 10 minutes' walk away from the main shopping area. The owners had been disturbed night after night by the sound of a young girl weeping in a particularly distressed manner. They described it as 'an anguished crying sound'. I visited their home in order to establish whether I could assist them with their problem.

On arriving at the house I walked through the small rooms but could detect nothing in particular that would lead me to believe that the home was experiencing negative visitation from a spirit entity. It was only when I was sitting in the small front sitting room that I heard for myself the noise they had described. It was indeed the sound of a young girl sobbing uncontrollably, but there was also a definite tone of terror in her cries.

I detected that the noise was coming from the hall-way and in particular just by the front door. I approached the door and opened it. I looked down towards my feet and there lay the spirit outline of a young girl aged around nine years. The clothes she wore – or what was left of them – were ragged and dirty and her legs were smeared with blood. As she lay brokenly on the doorstep I could feel her sense of fear and humiliation.

'The child has been raped repeatedly,' I heard Sam's voice tell me. 'Her name is Susie.'

I gained the impression that this horrendous act had taken place many, many years ago. Sam went on to tell me that in the nineteenth century there was a fallacy that sexual relations with a virgin child were a cure for the venereal diseases prevalent at that time. Susie had fallen prey to a man who had contracted a sexually transmitted disease and wished to rid himself of it. He had waylaid her on her way home from play and had subjected her to this awful attack, as a result of which she had bled to death on the doorstep of her home.

'Please help me, mister,' I heard the young girl's voice plead between her sobs. 'I'm lost and I need me mam.'

I asked Sam to help me send the child over to the light and it was with great satisfaction that I saw a woman from the spirit world enter the light and scoop up young Susie. No longer would she cry out in hurt and shame. She was safe in the care of the spirit world.

Another young victim was Alice, whose spirit I met whilst working near Blackburn. Although Alice's spirit had found its way to the higher side of life, she was unsettled. The man who had murdered her had suffocated her and left her body at the scene of the crime in the vicinity of a local park. Although only nine years of age when she left her physical life, Alice was upset that nobody had ever been brought to justice. Her spirit would return time and time again to the area surrounding the park and had been witnessed by numerous people, who reported seeing a poorly dressed young girl looking lost and upset. When they approached her to offer help, she would disappear as though into thin air.

I went along to communicate with the spirit of Alice in an attempt to persuade her to allow herself to move on and progress in the world of spirit. I tried to explain to her that holding on to past misdeeds, no matter how terrible, was doing nothing other than hindering her own progression.

I would like to think that I was successful in my endeavours, as no more sightings of Alice have been reported.

Of course not all spirit children who remain grounded have lost their physical lives through violence. Some have passed over to the spirit world as a result of sickness and have somehow lost their way during that transition and have not arrived properly at their place in the higher side of life.

One such spirit child was Anne, whom I met whilst conducting an investigation at Tongue Hall, near Manchester. She had remained in the bedroom of the old house, afraid to move away and upset by what she considered her abandonment by her family. She was also frightened and confused by the changing faces over the passing years.

Upon my arrival in the bedroom that she had occupied for so long, I recognized that she was lost and needed to be sent to join her mother in the light. With the help of the people with whom I was working, this was done. Anne's mother collected her daughter and took her to her rightful place in the heavenly side of life.

It has always been my practice, without exception, that when I happen across a location where there is a lost soul, a child or otherwise, I do my best to assist that spirit to complete their transition and join their family in the heavenly state.